REGIONAL FAVORITES ~ FROM ~ EAST TO WEST AND ~ NORTH TO SOUTH

UNITED STATES of PIE

ADRIENNE KANE

ILLUSTRATIONS BY AUGUST HEFFNER

ecco
An Imprint of HarperCollins Publishers

Also by Adrienne Kane

Cooking and Screaming

UNITED STATES OF PIE. Copyright © 2012 by Adrienne Kane. All rights reserved. Printed in the United States of America. No part of this book may be used or reproduced in any manner whatsoever without written permission except in the case of brief quotations embodied in critical articles and reviews. For information address HarperCollins Publishers, 10 East 53rd Street, New York, NY 10022.

HarperCollins books may be purchased for educational, business, or sales promotional use. For information please write: Special Markets Department, HarperCollins Publishers, 10 East 53rd Street, New York, NY 10022.

Library of Congress Cataloging-in-Publication Data has been applied for.

ISBN: 978-0-06-206407-3

12 13 14 15 16 IND/QGT 10 9 8 7 6 5 4 3 2

For my father

Pie is swell food. I eat scads of it. I have a good complexion and marvelous digestion. I always tell people who say pie gives them indigestion to try eating pie first and the rest of the meal last.

—"PIE KING" MONROE BOSTON STRAUSE,
JEFFERSON CITY POST-TRIBUNE,
DECEMBER 16, 1937

CONTENTS

Crusts for Every Pie

As American as Apple Pie *47*

Pies of the Northeast

Pies of the South

Pies of the Midwest

Pies of the West

ACKNOWLEDGMENTS

During the writing of this book, there were many individuals who lent support, guidance, knowledge, talent, appetite, laughter, intelligence, love, a cup of sugar, a critical eye, or a discerning palate. I will be forever indebted to each of you: Dan Halpern, Libby Edelson, Alia Habib, August Heffner, Suet Chong, Irene Bouchard, Cindy Trezciak, Jeni Makepeace, Jen Biddle, Larrick Martin, Andy Case, the Duartes, Karen Handler, Jennifer Sahadi, Ian Quinn, Aaron Hyman, and, as always, Brian Kane. I owe each of you a slice of pie.

INTRODUCTION

After my husband, Brian, and I moved from Manhattan to New Haven, Connecticut, it seemed like I became instantly homesick. Not for New York City, though, but for Northern California, where I grew up. Moving from one place to another on the East Coast, rather than moving back West again, made our new address seem all the more permanent. This was where I lived now. But was New Haven home?

Homesickness manifests itself in funny ways. For me, I was drawn to the place that had always been a source of warmth, comfort, and a sense of accomplishment: the kitchen. But instead of cooking innovative modern food as per my usual habits, I pulled out the biceps-curling cast-iron Dutch oven that had been in my family for years. Potatoes were now my friends. I slathered whole chickens in butter and roasted them in a slow oven. *I* had never cooked this way before, but it was still deeply familiar to me—this was the home cooking of my late grandmother and of her childhood on a South Dakota farm.

Such homey meals demanded a homey dessert, and for me, that meant pie. Pie solved two of my problems in one fell swoop: it kept my sweet tooth happy (there's nothing like sugar for homesickness), and it reminded me of my own culinary traditions. My grandma was one of those women who could whip up a pie with one hand tied behind her back, never using a measuring cup or a proper teaspoon. I can't even tell you when I ate my first slice of pie—I just know that it was my grandma's.

Every year, come Thanksgiving morning, my grandma would pull up at our house, popping the "pie trunk" of her massive Crown Victoria as she slowed to a stop in the driveway. Pie after pie sat in Grandma's trunk, nestled between kitchen towels and aprons that rendered the stacks impervious to the rocking of the vehicle. There would be blueberry, sweet and staining, and strawberry-rhubarb with rivulets of juice creeping out over the crust, both made with fruit my grandma froze at the peak of the season. Classic apple pie sat next to rich pumpkin, its custard cracked during baking from the heat of the oven. We carried the pies to the laundry room—the only place with room to house these numerous desserts—and covered them with cotton dish towels. Throughout Thanksgiving dinner, my appetite wandered to what waited for me at the end of the meal. The turkey was just a precursor to the main event.

With one woman's stellar baking skills so readily at hand, there was little need for me to learn how to bake a pie myself. My grandma was generous with her sugar—if I hankered for a pie, I had only to ask. And many times I kept her company as she made her famous pies. I watched her cut fats into flour; I watched her peel and slice apples with the same dull paring knife; I watched her crimp her crusts and vent her pies. But for all that, until I moved to Connecticut, I had never baked a pie of my own. My entrance into pie making wasn't totally smooth. My crusts were patchy, my fluting uneven. Meringues wept and custards refused to set. But, just like speaking a foreign language, the more I practiced, the better I got.

Making a new home is as much about becoming acquainted with your new environment as it is about getting settled. So, those first months in Connecticut, when I wasn't braising a pot roast or rolling out rounds of dough, I found myself wandering the stacks of Sterling Memorial Library at Yale University. We had moved to New Haven because Brian had been offered a teaching job at Yale. Although I wasn't a student, his job meant that I had access to the libraries, and the only other activity that distracted me from my homesickness as much as baking was reading. At first I just wandered the stacks, thumbing the spines of dusty books. The stacks reminded me of a morgue, or at least how I imagined a morgue would look and feel: the ceiling was low, the lights flickered, and there was an ever-present chill. One day, Brian suggested that I take a look at the library's cookbook holdings. It had never occurred to me that a university library would even *have* a cookbook collection, there among the treatises on philosophy and critical theory.

I didn't waste any time. The next day, I headed straight for the stacks that housed the cookbooks, excited to check out some big, inspiring books full of lush photography and tantalizing recipes. But the cookbooks lining the shelves looked nothing like that. Instead of the glossy doorstoppers filled with color-saturated photographs that I was used to, few of these cookbooks even had dust jackets. Their spines were worn; some were even spiral-bound. Their pages were yellowed and softened.

I pulled a stack of books at random from the shelves. I dropped my satchel on the floor and sat down beside it, leaning my back against a bare wall. That first day I read for hours, completely lost in the cookbooks. There were books written *by* farmwives *for* farmwives, housekeeping guides, cooking manuals for newlywed brides, books produced by church groups and ladies' auxiliaries. Many of them had not been checked out in years, decades even—if ever. They were so much more than collections of recipes; each one was a little window into a world now gone, a historical record. By reading *Mrs. Porter's New Southern Cookery Book* from 1871, I learned how she culled a chicken and how she boiled the lightest, most tender dumplings. I was able to catch a glimpse of what her everyday life entailed.

Although many of the books were more than a century old, they somehow still seemed so modern. The recipes were based on local, seasonal ingredients. Many of the books contained chapters on canning and preserving. "Nose to tail" dishes were common. These weren't fashionable books, though. They were sensible, aimed at women who—usually by necessity—valued economizing, women who avoided waste, who had to make do with the ingredients available where they lived. And the result, almost as though by accident, was nourishing, soul-satisfying food. They showed that our culinary past was not about convenience food or TV dinners. It was about simmering, sautéing, and baking real food for family and friends.

I checked out a few of the books that struck me as most interesting and headed home, eager to spend some quality kitchen time with the pie recipes in particular. The recipes proved to be more challenging than I expected; I was used to modern cookbooks that were specific in every detail. Reading these recipes was more like cooking alongside an experienced grandmother. There was no mention of teaspoon measurements for spices, no oven temperatures indicated, no cooking times given, no fuss.

While the recipes intrigued me—the Avocado Pie from California certainly sounded delicious, if a little unfamiliar, and just reading about the Peanut Pie from Virginia or the Burnt Sugar Meringue Pie from Kansas was enough to make my stomach rumble—I could see how they would be mystifying and at times intimidating to cooks today. We have become accustomed to recipes with lists of ingredients, concise instructions, timetables, and, most certainly, suggested oven temperatures! It was no wonder so many of these cookbooks had not been checked out of the library in years. The recipes could use some updating, a bit of culinary excavation. A little less sugar, lighter spicing, more fruit, and these pies could enjoy a resurgence; they could truly become heirlooms of our culinary past to be celebrated. My experimentation began, many sacks of flour were bought, pounds of sugar were gone through, and the *United States of Pie* was born.

Think of this book as a jumping-off point into the world of pie. For the novice there are helpful hints, a chapter about making crusts, and a Getting Started guide to ingredients. For the experienced baker, this book is an invitation to do some culinary digging—there are plenty of unique and delectable pie recipes to be discovered here. Where the farmwife and the homemaker of yore left off, I have picked up! A combination of new and old, this book has recipes for tasty classics as well as new pies that I have come to delight in over the past few years. These recipes celebrate the remarkable foods of our land.

I am hardly the first person who has written about pie. Many people have done so before me, and therein lies the beauty of this book. The recipes that inspired this collection come from across the United States and span time. They were written by county fair winners and restaurant cooks alike. They were eaten at weekly church suppers or as favorite holiday desserts. They offer a way of experiencing our shared culinary heritage. So tie on an apron and grab your trusty rolling pin—there's no better time than the present to follow in the floury footsteps of the creative, resourceful men and women who came before us. It is time to create your own future legacy from our culinary past!

GETTING STARTED

For the most part, you won't find too many unusual ingredients in this cookbook. We're making pie here, not building rocket ships! You may even be able to make a pie or two without having to set foot in a market. Now that's what I call American ingenuity! But there are a few things to note.

FLOUR

The flour in these recipes is all-purpose, unless otherwise noted. All-purpose flour is a blend of hard and soft wheat that gives pie dough a reliable structure. It is sturdy yet tender, and easy to work with. It comes in bleached and unbleached varieties, and in this book you can use either. Whole wheat flour, which you will find in the Whole Wheat Pie Dough recipe (page 40), is simply flour that is milled with the germ and the bran still attached. It tends to be stiffer and coarser than all-purpose flour, and has a nuttier flavor.

GIVE ME SOME SUGAR

It seems that nowadays there are almost as many ways to sweeten desserts as there are desserts to bake. I am a purist.

You won't find a recipe in this book that uses a difficult-to-find sweetener, and I never use artificial sweeteners—they just leave a metallic aftertaste in your mouth (lick a penny!). But here are some sugars, and an explanation of what makes each so sweet.

Granulated sugar: This is the standard sugar, also called table sugar. The most common form of sugar, it is essentially sucrose, a carbohydrate that exists in virtually all fruits and vegetables.

Castor/caster sugar: Also a granulated sugar, this sugar simply has an extra-fine grain. It melts quicker and therefore is often used in meringues. It can be used interchangeably with table sugar.

Confectioners' sugar/powdered sugar: This sugar is ground several times to a powdery consistency. It is then mixed with cornstarch to prevent caking and clumping. Confectioners' sugar is used when making glazes or royal icing (a combination of egg white and confectioners' sugar). Given its powdery texture, this sugar also is ideal for dusting a decorative coating over many desserts.

Turbinado/Demerara sugar: Although these two raw sugars are not identical, they can be used interchangeably. Both are coarse sugars, with a large crystal and a light brown hue; they are made when the molasses, a naturally occurring component in sugar, is not skimmed out. These harder, coarse crystals melt slowly, making turbinado and Demerara ideal for sprinkling on cookies or pies before baking.

Sanding/decorating sugar: This is an even larger form of coarse sugar crystals. It is made when sugar syrup is crystallized, and is high in sucrose. It doesn't melt easily, leaving behind a sugary crunch, and is ideal for decorating and for sprinkling on a dessert before baking.

Brown sugar: In brown sugar, some amount of molasses is added during processing. The sugar is moist and has a lingering butterscotch flavor. Dark brown sugar contains more molasses and is richer in flavor than light brown sugar. In these recipes, light and dark brown sugar can be used interchangeably unless otherwise indicated. For example, I specify dark brown sugar for pies where a deeper caramel flavor is desired. The depth of flavor and richness of color in dark brown sugar also make it ideal in desserts such as mincemeat. When measuring brown sugar for these recipes, always pack it firmly in the measuring cup.

EGGS

I use large eggs. Organic eggs are recommended, especially in those pies that contain raw or not fully cooked eggs.

BUTTER

The butter in all of these recipes is unsalted. In baking I recommend using unsalted rather than salted butter. It's better to start with a neutral palate and add your own salt and other flavorings to it. That way you can determine exactly how much salt is needed.

MILK AND CREAM

When I call for milk I mean full-fat milk (whole milk), and when I call for cream I mean heavy cream. This is for a variety of reasons—primarily for flavor and texture. I always keep a carton of whole milk in my refrigerator. Whether you want to sit down with a frosty glass of whole milk is up to you, but it is the only choice for baking. Thicker, richer, and fuller in taste, whole milk offers a neutral flavor with a higher percentage of butterfat, which helps custards and puddings come together.

Cream is simply the fat that rises to the top of a bottle of non-homogenized milk. If you have ever been to a dairy farm, or purchased milk at a farmers' market, perhaps you've noticed the thick, yogurtlike shell protecting the milk—that is the cream. When my grandma was growing up on a farm in South Dakota, she had access to pure, unadulterated cream. Today it is becoming increasingly hard to find. At the grocery store most of the cream we buy is pasteurized or ultra-pasteurized, meaning it has been heated in order to kill disease-causing organisms and to prolong its shelf life. Because of the heating it can have a slightly cooked taste and often lacks that fresh, creamery taste of whole cream.

While there is more than one type of cream available, the recipes in this book call for heavy cream. Heavy cream contains anywhere from 36 to 40 percent butterfat. It is highly stable, thick, and rich. When whipped into peaks, heavy cream will hold its shape longer than whipping cream, which may contain only 30 to 36 percent butterfat. Never buy light cream thinking you can whip it. Light cream offers a smooth taste, but it does not have enough butterfat to hold peaks.

After all, if you are going to make a pie, make the best-tasting pie you can! Go on, use the whole milk, use the heavy cream. I guarantee the pie won't even be there long enough for you to feel guilty.

SALT

The salt in these pies is kosher salt. With its coarse grain, there is less salt per spoonful than with table salt. I also really appreciate the rough texture of kosher salt; it is similar to sea salt. While it mixes with the other ingredients well, it's pleasing to get those little bits of salty crunch in your piecrust.

WHAT ABOUT PIE PLATES?

All the pies in this book are made in 9-inch pie plates. This is the standard—not too big, not too small. As you might imagine, I have quite a few pie plates: metal (and disposable aluminum foil), ceramic, and, of course, Pyrex. They all have their merits, but usually I find myself returning to my Pyrex plates. A plain old Pyrex pie plate may not be the fanciest looking of the bunch, but it's the workhorse of any baker's kitchen.

My grandma used metal pie plates, and they are lightweight and usually inexpensive. The downside of metal pie plates is that typically they're made of aluminum, which can react badly with acidic fruit fillings, potentially creating off-flavors if the juices in the pie bubble over. And metal pie plates don't heat evenly, which can lead to a pie crust that is blotchy, not evenly golden brown. If you are committed to using this type of pie plate, look for the ones that have a dark interior surface—this helps the pan retain its heat.

If you're looking for a glitzy pie plate, one that is brightly colored and has a delicately fluted edge, ceramic is the way to go. However, while ceramic retains heat more efficiently than glass or metal, I've found that ceramic pie plates are slow to heat up. You may find that the pies baked in a ceramic dish actually need a longer time in the oven to get that burnished finish. Ceramic dishes tend to be the most expensive as well.

This leads us to the Pyrex pie plate. This oven-safe glass—which is so durable it's used in spacecrafts—heats up and retains that heat beautifully. Pyrex dishes are fairly inexpensive and can even be found in most grocery stores. Another plus in the Pyrex column? For the inexperienced baker, the transparent dish means it's extra easy to check the underside of the piecrust for browning and doneness. Just as a warning: Pyrex pans can suffer from thermal shock, or cracking, due to extreme temperature change. They also scratch, so if you are a frequent baker, it might be better to use a ceramic or metal pie plate. Then again, while writing this book, I tested and retested several pies a week in a good old Pyrex pan without any problems—and I would say that earns me the "frequent baker" title!

HOW TO MAKE THE PERFECT DOUGH

With few exceptions, I do not believe that machines should be used to make pie dough. Although they are handheld, I don't even subscribe to the dueling knives method, or to using a pastry cutter, for incorporating fats into flour. Cool hands are what do it for me. Call me a sideshow charlatan claiming the power of laying on of hands, but I believe in the power of touch. Making dough is a sensory experience. It is also imperfect. By touching the flour and manually working in the fats, you ensure that the result is an irregular, nubby mass. Irregularity is what you want! Pockets of fat melt when baked, and this uneven texture in the dough leads to a light, flaky finished crust.

Putting together a pie's filling is usually pretty elementary—we all can toss fruit and spices together, or mix ingredients to make custard. It's making the crust that seems to intimidate people and prevent them from baking pies from scratch. I understand. The only thing that I can say is that it takes practice—but not an inordinate amount of practice. You may have to make a few pies before you really get the rhythm of it. You may have to make one pie on a cold day and another one on a humid day before you figure out how much water you need to add to the dough so that it's workable yet not so moist that it will stick to the counter when you roll it out. But the thing is, pies are a lot like French fries: even a bad one is still pretty darn good. Each pie you bake will offer both a lesson and a delicious reward.

We all know what we want in a piecrust: a flaky and tender crumb that is also crisp, meltingly so. A golden-brown hue that announces that this pie has just seen the inside of an oven. A pleasingly bland flavor that's never in competition with the filling and a saltiness that balances the sweetness of the filling.

Flour and fat, a bit of salt, a sprinkling of sugar . . . sounds easy enough. It's how you handle these simple ingredients that makes all the difference. Here are some helpful hints that I have learned throughout my baking escapades. Read through them, roll up your sleeves, tie your apron strings, and get to making dough!

DRY INGREDIENTS

The dry ingredients—meaning flour, salt, and sugar—lay the foundation for a good dough. You can play with your dry ingredients as much as you like. In fact, I give you permission to do just that. Some cooks sift this mixture, others stir a whisk through the dry ingredients, and some simply twirl a spoon around in the bowl. I recommend sifting or whisking in order to aerate the dry mixture. You want the crust to bake up light and flaky. The easiest way to ensure this is to separate the particles.

FATS

Long ago, when women began baking pies, there was one and one thing only that they used to make divine dough, and that was lard. But as our society became increasingly non-agrarian, vegetable shortening, a commercial ingredient, became favored for baking. Today there are many bakers who would never use something as pedestrian as shortening, and they favor butter instead. For beginning bakers, a combination of butter and vegetable shortening produces the best results. Here is why: butter equals flavor and shortening equals flakiness. Also, dough that has a bit of shortening in it will be more malleable and easier to roll out.

Cut the cold butter and the shortening into half-inch cubes. Add the cubes to the flour-salt-sugar mixture and toss well to coat. Then begin working the fat into gravelly, pea-size pieces. It's important to keep the fat cool, so you don't want to overwork it—the heat of your hands can melt the fat. Keeping the fat cool allows it to remain chunky, creating layers of flakiness in the finished product. By rubbing the mixture you're not only combining the fats and the flour, you're also incorporating air into the mixture. Pie dough likes air; it contributes to a light crust.

17

ICE WATER

Here is where it gets tricky. Prior to this point, you might look down at your bowl and think, *This is just a pile of pebbles.* And you'd be right. That pile of sandy pebbles needs liquid to become dough. Liquid and touch. This is the part of creating dough that makes people most nervous. You'll never see a dough recipe with exact amounts of liquid measurements. That's because making pie dough is not an exact science.

Remember all of those aerated particles that we created earlier? We want them to remain this way. The only way to do this is to keep them chilled, surrounding the particles with cold water while turning the mass into dough. You want to add enough liquid, but not too much.

KNEADING THE DOUGH

Now is the time to roll up your sleeves. As you drizzle in the ice water, knead the dough firmly and quickly. Don't worry about being delicate; dough is strong and resilient. This is where you have to take a deep breath, trust yourself, and rely on your senses.

Sight: You need to see the dough transform from a shaggy mess into a more cohesive mass.

Touch: Is your dough smooth but not sticky? If so, you are on the right track. When you first add water, the dough will become stickier, clinging to both your hands and the sides of the bowl. As you add more water, the mass will look more like dough and the sides of the bowl will become clean.

Sound: This is perhaps the most difficult hint to describe but the most valuable to use. As you are adding water, spoonful by spoonful, you should hear a *squish*. This soft squeak as you knead the water into the flour signals completion. It tells you that enough water has been added to just bring the dough together, and you should stop. Almost immediately.

At this point, you are just about finished. Place the dough on a sheet of plastic wrap. (Your bowl should be almost completely clean.) Wrap the dough in the plastic wrap, press it firmly into a disk shape, and place it in the fridge. Dough needs to rest so the gluten can relax, which makes rolling it out easier. The dough should remain in the refrigerator for a minimum of 1 hour before being rolled out. A batch of dough will last about 2 days in the refrigerator. It also freezes beautifully for up to 1 month, though you'll have to defrost it in the fridge before you can work with it.

ROLLING OUT THE DOUGH

If there is one thing that I want you to walk away with after reading this section, it is that flour is your friend. Use it—on your board, on your rolling pin, on your dough. If your dough is very sticky, throw a bit more flour around; it will never hurt.

You may read in food magazines or in other cookbooks that in order to make the perfect piecrust you have to roll out your dough on a marble surface, or that you need a silicone rolling pin, or that only a certain type of flour will do for dusting your work surface. To me, this is persnickety. I am here to tell you just the opposite. I have made pie in a two-foot-square kitchen in New York City. I have seen dough rolled out with an empty wine bottle. I have rolled out dough in the middle of a freezing cold winter and in the sweltering days of summer. Sure, some of my pies have turned out better than others, but each pie has been delicious in its own right. What type of rolling pin you use is a matter of *your* preference.

Rolling out dough is a matter of confidence. You have to show that round who's boss. You are the creator—go ahead and play God. Dough is not delicate. It needs to be beaten. Once you have adequately floured your work surface, place the disk of dough on it. Flour the dough. Voilà, you're ready to begin. The following tips should make the process easier.

- The step before rolling is beating. With the flour-dusted disk of dough before you, use the rolling pin to beat the dough along both its horizontal and vertical axes. This makes the dough more malleable for the rolling process. Don't be scared— let the dough have it! This step will also spread the dough out. Just make sure to do the beating fairly evenly. You do not want a severely misshapen round of dough.

Next, make sure your rolling pin is adequately floured, and then begin to roll from the center of the dough outward. Whatever movement is done on one side of the dough should also be done on the other. Use short, quick motions, picking up the rolling pin before you reach the edge of the dough. This will prevent the edges from getting too thin.

As you roll, pick the dough up often. This prevents sticking. It also allows you to dust the work surface with additional flour if needed. Just think how horrible it would be to roll out a round of dough only to have it stick to the counter and tear.

Rolling out pie dough is a process. If you are finding the dough particularly sticky as time passes, just add more flour!

Be fairly speedy. The longer the dough is out of the refrigerator, the stickier it can become—especially in the warm summer months. I find it easiest to prepare the filling prior to rolling out my dough. Or, if it is a single-crusted pie, I prepare the dough, crimp the edges, and then put the pie shell back into the refrigerator until the filling is ready.

Dough should be rolled out approximately ⅛-inch thick and wide enough to easily fit a 9-inch pie plate. This means that you should have a round of dough measuring 12 to 14 inches in diameter.

TRANSFERRING ROLLED DOUGH
TO A PIE PLATE

I find the easiest way to move the dough from the board and to the plate is with the rolling pin. If the dough is cool and loose (which it should be because you picked it up frequently during the rolling process), place the rolling pin on one edge and simply roll the pin, taking the dough with it. You will, in essence, be making a loose stocking of dough for your rolling pin. Pick up the pin, place an edge of dough at the edge of the pie plate, and unfurl the dough.

Another way of getting the rolled-out dough into the pie plate is to loosely fold the dough into fourths, like a handkerchief. Again, having a well-floured, non-sticky round of dough is crucial here. Simply pick up the folded dough, place it in the pie plate, and then unfold.

Here is a bit more about putting the dough into the pie plate:

- Never grease the pie plate; it's just not necessary. There should be plenty of butter and/or shortening in the dough, and an additional coating of butter would just make the dough wet and the pie rather slippery.

- Make sure that you fit the dough into the plate well, so that it is touching the entire surface.

- Trim the dough before fluting it. You want approximately a 1-inch overhang of dough draping over the edge of the pie plate.

FLUTING

The fluting is your opportunity to be creative. Or not. But before any fluting begins, it is necessary to turn under the cut edge of the dough, gently pressing it into the lip of the pie plate, creating a raised edge. This step is especially important when baking a double-crusted pie, when you will be sealing the top crust to the bottom crust. Here are a few fluting techniques:

- The pinching method is a classic, and can be done either one- or two-handed. For the one-handed method, make a tripod shape with your thumb, index, and middle finger, with about an inch between each finger. With the index and middle finger on the inner lip of dough and the thumb on the outer, pinch the dough into a zigzag shape. Repeat until the entire dough is crimped, using one crimp as a guide for the next.

- For the two-handed method, put your left hand on the outer lip of the pie, in a pinching shape with two fingers held about a penny's diameter apart. With the right hand on the inner lip of the pie, press the dough into the left hand, creating the same zigzag shape. Repeat as above.

- For an easier fluting method, simply push the dough down so it is evenly covering the lip of the pie plate. Take a fork and use the tines to indent the dough all along the perimeter of the pie plate.

- ❧ The final technique is really a non-technique. For a relatively smooth finish, keep the dough turned under and up: plain and simple.

MISCELLANEOUS TIPS

When baking a double-crusted pie, I have found it important to gently make an indention around the edge of the filling, pressing on the surface of the dough. This prevents a certain amount of leakage and creates a vessel in which the fruit steams and bakes into a syrupy, glossy filling. It is also important to vent a double-crusted pie. This allows steam to escape, ensuring that the filling does not get watery.

Sometimes a double-crusted fruit pie leaks, no matter how careful you've been. To prevent a messy oven and a smoky kitchen, I often place my unbaked pie on a baking sheet before slipping it into the oven.

Painting the surface of a double-crusted pie with a bit of heavy cream adds a lovely sheen to the baked pie. If you use the cream, also feel free to sprinkle sugar over the unbaked pie. As the pie bakes, the sugar caramelizes, and it will crackle when you slice a wedge of freshly baked pie.

Now let's get going. There are pies to be made!

CRUSTS for EVERY PIE

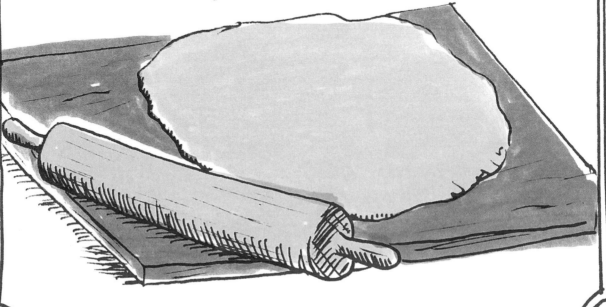

Most of the recipes in this chapter make two rounds of dough—enough for one double-crusted pie. When dough for a single-crusted pie is called for, simply freeze the other half for use later.

Standard Pie Dough

Good pie dough is an exercise in balance. You want it to be flaky yet buttery, crisp yet substantial, salty yet sweet. That's a lot of requirements for one lump of dough, and this is the recipe that will deliver just what you are seeking. This dough is especially friendly to beginners.

Makes enough for one 9-inch double-crusted pie or two 9-inch pie shells

2 cups all-purpose flour
2 tablespoons sugar
1 teaspoon kosher salt
6 tablespoons unsalted butter, chilled, cut into ½-inch cubes
6 tablespoons vegetable shortening, chilled, cut into ½-inch cubes
6 to 10 tablespoons ice water

In a large bowl, whisk together the flour, sugar, and salt until well blended and free of lumps. Add the butter and the shortening and toss gently to coat. With your fingertips, work the fats into the flour, rubbing the larger pieces of butter and shortening between your fingers until the mixture resembles gravel.

Sprinkle on the water, 1 tablespoon at a time, starting with a total of 3 tablespoons and then gradually adding more water if needed. As you add the water, blend it in with your fingertips, as quickly as possible, pulling the mixture together and creating a dough. The dough will become less sticky and more of a mass when enough water has been added. Finally, knead the dough minimally in the bowl to make sure it has just enough moisture.

Divide the dough in half. (One mound of dough should weigh approximately 10½ ounces.) Place each half on a sheet of plastic wrap and seal it. Gently form each one into a disk roughly ¾-inch thick. Place the wrapped dough in the refrigerator and leave it for at least 1 hour, or up to 2 days, before rolling it out. The dough can be frozen for up to 1 month and defrosted in the refrigerator before using.

Rich and Buttery Pie Dough

I am not one of those bakers who swears off shortening; it has its merits. But there are times when I desire the richness of an all-butter crust, and when I do, this is the crust I turn to. All-butter piecrust can be a little finicky. While the same rules apply when making this dough—the colder the dough stays, the better—you may find the finished product difficult to roll out. The cold dough is too stiff, and needs to rest at room temperature before it can be easily played with. Leave it on the counter for around fifteen minutes prior to rolling. Butter dough doesn't hold crimping or fluting as well as shortening-butter dough. Know this going in, but don't fret: I guarantee a sumptuous-tasting final product.

Unlike standard pie dough, this dough is made with cold milk, an egg yolk, and a bit of cider vinegar. The milk lends the dough a richness that water can't, and the egg yolk further ups the ante and lends a sunny hue. The vinegar imparts tang and inhibits the gluten in the flour from forming, which ensures a flaky and flavorful crust.

Makes enough for one 9-inch double-crusted pie or two 9-inch pie shells

2 cups all-purpose flour

2 tablespoons sugar

1 teaspoon kosher salt

2 teaspoons apple cider vinegar

12 tablespoons (1½ sticks) unsalted butter, chilled, cut into ½-inch cubes

1 large egg yolk

¼ cup cold whole milk, plus a few extra tablespoons
    if needed

In a large bowl, whisk together the flour, sugar, and salt until well blended and free of lumps. Sprinkle in the vinegar and whisk again. Add the butter and toss gently to coat. With your fingertips, work the butter into the flour, rubbing the larger pieces of butter between your fingers until the mixture resembles gravel.

Beat the egg yolk with the ¼ cup cold milk until well combined. Pour the milk mixture into the flour mixture. Blend with your fingertips, as quickly as possible, pulling the mixture together and creating a dough. If the dough still feels dry after adding the milk mixture, add more cold milk, 1 tablespoon at a time, until the dough comes together. The dough will become less sticky and more of a mass when enough milk has been added. Finally, knead the dough minimally in the bowl to make sure it has just enough moisture.

Divide the dough in half. (One mound of dough should weigh approximately 11 ounces.) Place each half on a sheet of plastic wrap and seal it. Gently form each one into a disk roughly ¾-inch thick. Place the wrapped dough in the refrigerator and leave it for at least 1 hour, or up to 2 days, before rolling it out. The dough can be frozen for up to 1 month and defrosted in the refrigerator before using.

Remove the dough from the refrigerator 15 minutes prior to rolling.

Leaf Lard Pie Dough

Lard: one little ingredient that is fraught with such unpleasant connotations! Let me assure you that lard makes a crust so light, so flaky, so delicious, that you will be left wondering why this fat gets such a bad rap. Leaf lard is a virtually flavorless pork fat that was used in all pie dough a century ago. Bakers value leaf lard for creating layer upon layer of flaky dough. Dough made with this lard is meltingly tender, sturdy enough to hold its shape when baked, yet shatteringly crisp.

It is important to note that leaf lard is not standard commercial lard, which is often labeled manteca in the grocery store. Manteca is hydrogenated, contains trans fats, and is high in cholesterol. But leaf lard, often sold by butchers or at farmers' markets, contains a lower level of saturated fat than butter, and in fact contains an acceptable level of monounsaturated fat (the good fat).

When working with lard, you'll notice that it's very thick and rather sticky. When you work the lard into the flour, the texture will mellow as the heat of your hands warms the fat.

Makes enough for one 9-inch double-crusted pie or two 9-inch pie shells

2 cups all-purpose flour

2 tablespoons sugar

¾ teaspoon kosher salt

10 tablespoons (1¼ sticks) unsalted butter, chilled, cut into ½-inch cubes

¼ cup leaf lard, chilled, cut into ½-inch cubes

6 to 10 tablespoons ice water

In a large bowl, whisk together the flour, sugar, and salt until well blended and free of lumps. Add the butter and lard and toss gently to coat. With your fingertips, work the fats into the flour, rubbing the larger pieces of butter and lard until the mixture resembles gravel.

Sprinkle on the water, 1 tablespoon at a time, starting with a total of 3 tablespoons and then gradually adding more water if needed. Blend it in with your fingertips, as quickly as possible, pulling the mixture together and creating a dough. The dough will become less sticky and more of a mass when enough water has been added. Finally, knead the dough minimally in the bowl to make sure it has just enough moisture.

Divide the dough in half. (One mound of dough should weigh approximately 10½ ounces.) Place each half on a sheet of plastic wrap and seal it. Gently form each one into a disk roughly ¾-inch thick. Place the wrapped dough in the refrigerator and leave it for at least 1 hour, or up to 2 days, before rolling it out. The dough can be frozen for up to 1 month and defrosted in the refrigerator before using.

ABOUT LARD

What is sticky and smooth, off-white like a scoop of French vanilla ice cream, smells remotely like a barnyard yet tastes flavorless, and makes the lightest, flakiest pie dough imaginable? The substance is lard, and before gasping about trans fats and hydrogenation, let me tell you that lard is actually lower in saturated fat than butter and is 45 percent monounsaturated fat.

Lard is, simply put, rendered pork fat. The highest quality lard is leaf lard; it comes from the fat that surrounds a pig's kidneys. When this lard is rendered and cooled it is virtually flavorless, making it ideal for baking. When you hear people reminiscing about their grandmother's feather-weight pie dough made with lard, this is the lard they're talking about. Fatback is the next grade of lard; it comes from the back skin and muscle of the pig. In addition to giving off a moderate porcine fragrance, fatback often tastes slightly piggy.

In the nineteenth and early twentieth centuries in this country, pig was king. These barnyard animals had it good. They were plump, and roly-poly, and ate well. In turn, they were truly eaten from nose to tail. Chops, ribs, and loins were cooked. The lard was rendered, and it seemed that every refrigerator and pantry held containers of cooled and solidified lard. Then the industrial revolution came, and it became cheaper to produce vegetable oils. Society was becoming more urban and less agrarian. Highly stable vegetable shortenings (derived from vegetable oils) became prevalent. By the late twentieth century, animal fats had become taboo.

Today leaf lard and fatback are lumped together with the commercial-grade lard sold in grocery stores in 1-pound bricks or tubs. Commercial-grade lard is almost another beast entirely. This is the lard that, when eaten in abundance, leads to obesity. For stability reasons, commercial-grade lard is hydrogenated, making it full of unhealthy trans fats and bad cholesterol.

So if you are looking to make the flakiest and most healthful pie dough you can, you need to get your hands on some leaf lard. While this type of lard *is* becoming more readily available, you may just have to render it yourself.

Rendering only sounds frightening. Basically, when you render lard, you're cooking the fat down to a liquid form and then allowing it to cool into a solid form. Pork fat scorches easily, so it is necessary to melt the fat at a low temperature. This can be done one of two ways: either on the stovetop or in the oven.

Though a lot depends on the quality and type of lard you're going to render, you should get approximately 1 cup of rendered lard per 1 pound of leaf lard. Tightly sealed, lard keeps for several months in the refrigerator and can be frozen successfully.

To render lard on the stovetop, first cut the fat into small bits. Cook the fat in a Dutch oven over low heat. The fat will begin to liquefy fairly quickly. Continue cooking for 1 to 2 hours, stirring occasionally. The water in the fat will evaporate, and the fat will bubble and percolate. When the boiling becomes sluggish, remove the pot from the heat and strain the fat through a cheesecloth-lined strainer into a container with a tight-fitting lid. The crispy bits left behind in the strainer are cracklings; the strained liquid is the lard. Cool the lard completely; then cover and refrigerate.

You may also choose to render the lard in the oven. Preheat the oven to 250°F. Cut the lard into 1-inch cubes and place them in a Dutch oven. Add ¼ cup of water per 1 pound of lard to the Dutch oven. (The water ensures that the lard will not scorch before it liquefies.) Place the Dutch oven in the preheated oven. Cook the lard, stirring it every 30 minutes, until the water evaporates and the lard has exuded much of its liquid fat. This can take 2 to 4 hours. Strain the liquid lard through a cheesecloth-lined strainer into a container. Cool the lard completely, and then seal tightly and refrigerate.

Sour Cream Pie Dough

This dough is light yet rich, with a hint of tanginess from the sour cream. I especially like it with rich, stand-out winter pies such as pumpkin or mincemeat (see pages 72, 87).

Makes enough for one 9-inch double-crusted pie or two 9-inch pie shells

2 cups all-purpose flour

2 tablespoons sugar

¾ teaspoon kosher salt

8 tablespoons (1 stick) unsalted butter, chilled, cut into ½-inch cubes

4 tablespoons (¼ cup) vegetable shortening, chilled, cut into ½-inch cubes

½ cup sour cream

2 to 5 tablespoons ice water

In a large bowl, whisk together the flour, sugar, and salt until well blended and free of lumps. Add the butter and the shortening, and toss gently to coat. Add the sour cream. With your fingertips, work the fats into the flour, rubbing them into the flour until the mixture resembles gravel.

Sprinkle on the ice water, 1 tablespoon at a time, starting with a total of 2 tablespoons and then gradually adding more water if needed. Blend with your fingertips, as quickly as possible, pulling the mixture together and creating a dough. The dough will become less sticky and more of a mass when enough water has been added. Finally, knead the dough minimally in the bowl to make sure it has just enough moisture.

Divide the dough in half. (One mound of dough should weigh approximately 11 ounces.) Place each half on a sheet of plastic wrap and seal it. Gently form each one into a disk roughly ¾-inch thick. Place the wrapped dough in the refrigerator and leave it for at least 1 hour, or up to 2 days, before rolling it out. The dough can be frozen for up to 1 month and defrosted in the refrigerator before using.

Cornmeal Pie Dough

This recipe is very similar to the Standard Pie Dough on page 28. It is easy to roll, does not shrink, and holds its fluting quite well. The one major difference is the addition of a bit of fine-grained cornmeal, which gives the finished piecrust more body, a slightly gritty texture, and a nutty taste. This crust is ideal paired with many of the summer fruit pies, such as the peach or apricot-ginger (see pages 104, 184), and all the berry pies.

Makes enough for one 9-inch double-crusted pie or two 9-inch pie shells

1¾ cups all-purpose flour

¼ cup fine stone-ground cornmeal

2 tablespoons sugar

1 teaspoon kosher salt

6 tablespoons unsalted butter, chilled, cut into ½-inch cubes

6 tablespoons vegetable shortening, chilled, cut into ½-inch cubes

6 to 10 tablespoons ice water

In a large bowl, whisk together the flour, cornmeal, sugar, and salt until well blended and free of lumps. Add the butter and the shortening, and toss gently to coat. With your fingertips, work the fats into the flour mixture, rubbing the larger pieces of butter and shortening between your fingers until the mixture resembles gravel.

Sprinkle on the ice water, 1 tablespoon at a time, starting with a total of 3 tablespoons and then gradually adding more water if needed. Blend it in with your fingertips, as quickly as possible, pulling the mixture together and creating a dough. The dough will become less sticky and more of a mass when enough water has been added. Finally, knead the dough minimally in the bowl to make sure it has just enough moisture.

Divide the dough in half. (One mound of dough should weigh approximately 10½ ounces.) Place each half on a sheet of plastic wrap and seal it. Gently form each one into a disk roughly ¾-inch thick. Place the wrapped dough in the refrigerator and leave it for at least 1 hour, or up to 2 days, before rolling it out. The dough can be frozen for up to 1 month and defrosted in the refrigerator before using.

Whole Wheat Pie Dough

Made with a combination of whole wheat flour and all-purpose flour, this dough is sturdier and a bit weightier than standard pie dough. It has a more rustic feeling as a result of the coarser whole wheat flour, and a pleasantly nutty flavor that I really like. Because the flour is coarser, you might find the crust more difficult to roll out to the typical ⅛-inch thickness. It's fine to leave the dough slightly thicker than you would normally; it will still bake up light and flaky.

Makes enough for one 9-inch double-crusted pie or two 9-inch pie shells

1¾ cups all-purpose flour
½ cup whole wheat flour
2 tablespoons sugar
1 teaspoon kosher salt
8 tablespoons (1 stick) unsalted butter, chilled, cut into ½-inch cubes
6 tablespoons vegetable shortening, chilled, cut into ½-inch cubes
6 to 10 tablespoons ice water

In a large bowl, whisk together the flours, sugar, and salt until well blended and free of lumps. Add the butter and the shortening, and toss gently to coat. With your fingertips, work the fats into the flour, rubbing the larger pieces of butter and shortening between your fingers until the mixture resembles gravel.

Sprinkle on the water, 1 tablespoon at a time, starting with a total of 3 tablespoons and then gradually adding more water if needed. Blend with your fingertips, as quickly as possible, pulling the mixture together and creating a dough. The dough will become less sticky and more of a mass when enough water has been added. Finally, knead the dough minimally in the bowl to make sure it has just enough moisture.

Divide the dough in half. (One mound of dough should weigh approximately 11 ounces.) Place each half on a sheet of plastic wrap and seal it. Gently form each one into a disk roughly ¾-inch thick. Place the wrapped dough in the refrigerator and leave it for at least 1 hour, or up to 2 days, before rolling it out. The dough can be frozen for up to 1 month and defrosted in the refrigerator before using.

Graham Cracker Crust

A little bit sweet, a little bit oaty, and slightly crumbly, a graham cracker crust is a nice alternative to standard pie dough when making a single-crusted pie. Especially good with cream and meringue pies, a graham cracker crust somehow feels lighter than the typical short crust.

Makes one 9-inch piecrust

1¼ cups (5 ounces) graham cracker crumbs (approximately 1 sleeve of graham crackers)
2 tablespoons sugar
¼ teaspoon kosher salt
5 tablespoons unsalted butter, melted

Preheat the oven to 350°F.

In a medium-size bowl, mix together the graham cracker crumbs, sugar, salt, and butter until the mixture is evenly moist and the crumbs have darkened slightly and begun to clump together. Pour the mixture into a pie plate. Using your hands, press and flatten the crumb mixture evenly over the bottom of the plate, working it up to cover the sides as well. Press firmly; there should not be any cracks or holes in the crust.

Bake for 8 to 10 minutes, or until the crust is beginning to brown at the edges.

Vanilla Wafer Crust

Like a graham cracker crust, a vanilla wafer crust offers a crispy crunch that I like to pair with smooth, creamy fillings. It is especially delectable with banana cream pie (see page 138). When making this crust, don't skimp on the salt; it elevates the flavor while adding that salty-sweet element.

1⅓ cups (6 ounces) vanilla wafer (such as Nilla wafer) crumbs
½ teaspoon kosher salt
4 tablespoons (½ stick) unsalted butter, melted

Makes one 9-inch piecrust

Preheat the oven to 325°F.

In a medium-size bowl, mix together the wafer crumbs, salt, and butter until the mixture is evenly moistened and the crumbs have darkened slightly and begun to clump together. Pour the mixture into a pie plate. Using your hands, press and flatten the crumb mixture evenly over the bottom of the plate, working it up to cover the sides as well. Press firmly; there should not be any cracks or holes in the crust.

Bake for 13 to 15 minutes, or until the crust is beginning to brown at the edges.

Gingersnap Crust

Spicy and crunchy, this crust, made from crisp, store-bought gingersnap cookies, is an aromatic alternative to the graham cracker crust. Try this crust with citrus-flavored fillings, such as the Meyer Lemon Cream Pie (page 213). The warm, perfumed flavor of the gingersnaps adds an extra brightness to creamy pies.

Makes one 9-inch piecrust

1¼ cups (5 ounces) gingersnap crumbs
¼ teaspoon kosher salt
4 tablespoons (½ stick) unsalted butter, melted

Preheat the oven to 350°F.

In a medium-size bowl, mix together the gingersnap crumbs, salt, and butter until the mixture is evenly moistened and the crumbs have darkened slightly and begun to clump together. Pour the mixture into a pie plate. Using your hands, press and flatten the crumb mixture evenly over the bottom of the plate, working it up to cover the sides as well. Press firmly; there should not be any cracks or holes in the crust.

Bake for 10 to 12 minutes, or until the crust is beginning to brown at the edges.

AS AMERICAN AS APPLE PIE

Whether you hail from California or Connecticut, Alabama or Idaho, chances are that at some point you've had a slice of apple pie for dessert. More than half of the states in the Union grow apples. From New York State's Ginger Gold to Braeburns from Washington or Honeycrisps from Minnesota, there is an apple that caters to each American's taste. Though this book is all about regional pies, it only makes sense to begin with the one pie that is quintessentially American. Apple pie is ingrained in our culture, part of our collective identity. Like hot dogs sizzling at a backyard barbecue, turkeys roasting to a golden hue at Thanksgiving, and gooey s'mores eaten next to a campfire, apple pie has become a culinary tradition, so much so that one-third of all Americans cite apple as their favorite kind of pie.

The phrase "as American as apple pie" is actually a shortened version of "as American as motherhood and apple pie." While everyone on earth has a mother (that's biology for you) and the apple pie originates in fact from England, not America, the saying is emblematic of a sentiment. This pie is meant to signal home (wherever that may be), family, warmth—all the attributes that we think of when we think of Mom. But this saying means more than just Mom. For me, apple pie exemplifies an essential feature of pie making—the transformation of a pile of ingredients into a beauti-

ful dessert. The apple pie isn't fussy: just a handful of fruit, gently tossed together, tumbled into a pie plate, and baked in a tempting crust. It is noble, simple, and unpretentious—kind of like Mom. You can eat apple pie in any state, in any town. Not affiliated with a holiday, nor eaten in any particular month, it is just plain good.

With this in mind, I knew that the apple pie in this book had to be a standout. So, in my search for the quintessential apple pie, I tested many recipes, with many different varieties of apples. In the end, I think a mix of apples yields the best results: you want to use baking apples for their body and tartness, and crunchy eating apples for their full flavor.

This pie makes me think of the first day of school, of leaves changing, of curling up on the couch with my feet ensconced in woolen socks, of my mom and of home. I wanted a classic. This is the pie that does it for me.

1 recipe Standard Pie Dough (page 28)

1¼ pounds (approximately 3 medium) baking apples, such as Granny Smith or Pippin, peeled, cored, and cut into ¼-inch-thick slices (4 cups)

14 ounces (approximately 2 medium) eating apples, such as Fuji or McIntosh, peeled, cored, and cut into ¼-inch-thick slices (3 cups)

Juice of ½ medium lemon

½ cup brown sugar

½ teaspoon ground cinnamon

⅛ teaspoon ground nutmeg, preferably freshly grated (see page 155)

Pinch of kosher salt

2 tablespoons all-purpose flour

2 tablespoons brandy

2 tablespoons unsalted butter, chilled, cut into
  ½-inch cubes

Optional

1 tablespoon heavy cream

1 tablespoon turbinado or sanding sugar

Preheat the oven to 425°F.

In a large bowl, gently toss the apple slices with the lemon juice, brown sugar, cinnamon, nutmeg, salt, flour, and brandy until thoroughly mixed. Set aside.

On a well-floured surface, roll out one portion of the dough until it is about ⅛-inch thick and will fit a 9-inch pie plate. Gently pick up the dough, center it over the pie plate, and ease it into the plate. Let the excess dough hang over the rim. Pour in the filling and spread it out evenly. Dot the apple mixture with the butter.

Roll out the second portion of dough to the same size. Lay the dough over the filling. Trim the edges of both layers of dough to leave a 1-inch overhang. Pressing the edges together, fold them under, and then decoratively crimp the perimeter. With a sharp knife, cut 5 vents in the top crust.

Bake the pie for 15 minutes. Then reduce the heat to 375° and continue baking for 45 to 50 minutes, until the crust is golden brown. Let the pie cool to room temperature before enjoying.

Optional:
For a lovely sheen on the baked pie, use a pastry brush to paint the surface with the cream. If you like, sprinkle the sugar over the cream. As the pie bakes, the sugar will caramelize, and it will crackle when you slice a wedge of the freshly baked pie.

PIES of the NORTHEAST

No regional cuisine in the United States

is more defined by the foods of the first European settlers than that of the Northeast. The English immigrants who landed on New England's coast had to adapt their recipes to capitalize on the available crops. From the thickets of Maine's wild blueberries to Massachusetts's cranberry bogs, the New World's bounty of indigenous fruits and vegetables was a huge boon to our culinary inheritance. What would Thanksgiving be without pumpkin pie and cranberry sauce?

But in true American fashion, European settlers would also come to adapt native crops through breeding and cultivation, creating new and unique varieties of fruits and vegetables such as the Concord grape, a cultivar of the fox grape, native to the Northeast. Developed in 1849 by Ephraim Bull Wales in—you guessed it—Concord, Massachusetts, Concord grapes are the über American grape, the grape of supermarket staples such as grape jelly and grape juice. They've just started making their way to supermarkets whole and unprocessed. However, their thick skins and high seed count make them a time-consuming fruit with which to cook—or even to snack on.

But one taste of a Concord grape pie will convince you they're worth the effort, and there's no better place to do just that than in Naples, New York. A small village in the Finger Lakes region, Naples is Concord grape country: vineyards lush with dusty grapevines line the roads into town; businesses along Route 21, Naples's main drag, fly flags advertising grape pies for sale; and sandwich boards dot the corners of the intersections, pointing the way toward home bakeshops. For more than forty years, the village has hosted the Naples Grape Festival every September, and the 1,500-person community swells with almost 100,000 visitors, there to wine and dine and eat slice after slice of homemade Concord grape pie.

New York is one of the few states in the country in which it's legal to operate a home bakeshop, allowing individuals—most of them women—to produce and sell small-batch baked goods from their home kitchens. For women like Irene Bouchard, Cindy Trezciak, and Jeni Makepeace, baking pies—especially Concord grape pies—is more than just a hobby or even a valued family tradition. These women are entrepreneurs whose home bakeshops—innovative small businesses built on hard work, pride, and community—have afforded them economic stability and independence.

Ninety-two-year-old Irene Bouchard is the grande dame of the grape pie, credited by locals as the Queen of Pies. Irene began baking Concord grape pies at the request of a local businessman, Al Hodges, owner of the Redwood Restaurant. In the early 1960s, Hodges added Concord grape pie to the Redwood's menu as a way to capitalize on the region's most famous product and to lure tourists. The pie was such a hit that demand for it quickly outstripped his kitchen's ability to produce them, so he hired Irene—who ran a home bakeshop just across the road—to pick up the slack.

Irene had always been a skilled home baker, but it wasn't

until the late 1950s, spurred on by her family and coworkers at the Widmer winery, that she decided to open a bakeshop. At that time there weren't any other bakeries in town, commercial or otherwise, and her bakeshop slowly took off. But everything changed when she began baking for the Redwood Restaurant. People started coming from miles around, hungry for grape pie, and a new local economy was born. By the 1980s, Irene was baking thousands of pies a year.

Though Irene stopped baking pies several years ago, she can still talk shop with the best of them. This downy-haired maven told me about the "floating crust," a technique that she developed as the popularity of her pies grew. She would roll and crimp only the bottom crust of the pie, pour in the thickened filling, then place a floating round of dough on top of the filling, leaving an open half-inch perimeter. This served as both a time-saver and a venting system. As the pies baked, pools of sticky filling bubbled up around the edges, seeping onto the surface of the pie. Ingenious!

As we sit and bond over our mutual love of pie, Irene shows me a scrapbook her daughter put together for her. In one yellowed photo, Irene's husband sits at their kitchen table–cum-workstation, surrounded by mounds of grapes. He was ready to help with what Naples-ites call "pinching"—releasing the pulp of the grapes from their loose skins. In another photo, a tour bus disgorges a horde of tourists in front of Irene's modest Victorian home. It hits me that these travelers were like me, excited to catch a glimpse of this local hero's home and eager to taste her pies.

We finish our visit in her lovingly kept and tidy kitchen, where everything has its place. Neatly organized jars of sugar, flour, and coffee line the counters and decorative wooden cutouts hang square and true on the walls. It's clear that this room has been well used and loved, churning out pie after pie, year after year. Though I've never been here before this day, I feel at home in this kitchen.

Women like Cindy Trezciak and Jeni Makepeace carry on Irene's legacy. Cindy is a Naples native, born and raised. Grapes are in her blood. Her home bakeshop, Cindy's Pies, sells 1,500 pies just over the course of the Naples Grape Festival alone. The recipe for her delicious pie has changed little in the thirty years that she's been baking it. She uses lard in her dough, just as her mother did, and tapioca to thicken the filling, just as she learned from her high school home economics teacher.

Despite the fact that she's been running the business for three decades now, she still seems surprised by her success. "I just thought we would do it for fun, and a little extra money for Christmas gifts," Cindy tells me. "You have to remember, we're just a bunch of hicks!" she says with a laugh. But I have to disagree. Cindy is kind, quick with both a compliment and a laugh, and though she may not think so, she is a shrewd businesswoman. When her husband was laid off and forced into early retirement, it was Cindy's Pies that kept the Trezciak family afloat—and does to this day. That seems like a viable business to me. Clearly, hundreds of people throughout the Finger Lakes region and beyond agree.

They keep coming back year after year for a slice of Cindy's grape pie.

Like Cindy Trezciak, Jeni Makepeace is a Naples lifer who started pie making as a way to augment her family's income. "I used to pinch for two pie bakers," says Jeni. "Then I thought, why just pinch? I should be making pies!" Ten years and three World's Greatest Grape Pie titles later, Jeni is one of the stars of the new generation of Naples home bakers. Although her business is seasonal, baking mostly during the festival weekend, she does some home baking for local inns and restaurants.

Jeni operates her home bakery out of an old farmhouse that she and her husband have been renovating for the past few years. "We're the one covered in Tyvek," she tells me over the phone, and I'm immediately charmed. When I pull up in front of the farmhouse, I don't see Jeni. A cluster of chickens root for nits and bugs in the damp soil of the front yard. A shaggy, red-haired mutt ambles out from around back, not to bark, but to nudge me with her muzzle. In a matter of moments, Jeni speeds up the driveway in an old VW van. She hops out from behind the wheel, bandana tied around her head, wearing a nubby woolen sweater that looks as if it has seen a pie or two be baked. Jeni immediately apologizes, smiling sheepishly, for her tardiness. I explain that I have been poking around, watching the Makepeace menagerie in her absence.

Jeni seems both pleased and relieved, shoos the mutt from the center walkway, and guides me through the dim farmhouse and into the modern kitchen. This was clearly the first room to be completed during the renovation. Mismatched kitchen chairs circle a worn wooden table. Next to the battered table stands a metal restaurant-quality table, where Jeni rolls out round after round of dough during pie-making season.

Unlike Irene or Cindy, Jeni uses vegetable oil to make her crusts, and only a bit of flour to thicken the filling. I love that each woman has her own particular recipe for making Concord grape pie. The variety in their methods reminds me that each pie is the end result of these women's traditions and histories, the lessons they learned from other bakers—their friends, sisters, mothers, and grandmothers.

For Jeni, Grape Festival weekend is a haul. The hours are long, but as Jeni describes baking late into the night, the pulp staining her hands, Eminem and gangsta rap booming from the stereo as a group of friends helps her assemble the hundreds of pies, it occurs to me that she's describing the modern-day equivalent of a quilting bee. These women gather together to socialize and to help one another out, producing a handcrafted heirloom product—just substitute a syrupy pie for the snugly quilt. "It's a neat community thing," Jeni says. "There are a lot of hands that go into making one pie."

I pulled out of Jeni's driveway, hens clucking behind me, profoundly grateful to have met her and the other home bakers of Naples. When I first arrived in Naples, the town—so quaint and so picturesque—struck me as frozen in time, straight out of a Norman Rockwell painting. Then I met Irene, Cindy, and Jeni, modern women whose lives are inextricably intertwined with the town. Each of them saw a niche in the market, and they gladly filled it with flour, sugar, lard, tapioca, vegetable oil, and, of course, lots of grapes.

As I glanced over my shoulder at the many boxes of pie stacked in my backseat (what, you didn't think that Cindy or Jeni would send me home empty-handed, did you?), I saw more than the delicious treats awaiting me at the end of my long drive. I saw a generosity of spirit in pie form. Each one of the women I met baked without constantly looking over her shoulder to see what the next big baker was up to. Each was confident in her ability, and pleased with the pies that she made. Later, biting into what would be my first slice of many, I found that this generosity of spirit was something you could taste; an extra sweetness in the filling, an extra tenderness in the crust.

Concord Grape Pie

Those who have never tried a Concord grape pie are in for a treat. For the diner who doesn't really enjoy grape-flavored foods, that's quite all right: the flavor of this pie is so entirely unique, it won't make a difference. The nearest pie I can equate it with is blackberry, without the seeds. Deep, almost opaque, chewy and tart from the skins, with only the subtle taste of grapes, this is a berry pie like no other. Yes, making the pulp is labor-intensive and a bit time-consuming, so I suggest making at least double the filling you need and freezing the extra. With the relatively short grape season from late summer to early fall, when you are savoring this stellar purple concoction in the dead of winter, you will be happy you did!

Serve this pie with a roll of paper towels nearby, and don't forget to remove your tablecloth first—this filling stains!

1 recipe Standard Pie Dough (page 28)

2½ cups prepared Concord grape pulp (see page 62)
¾ cup sugar
Pinch of kosher salt
Juice of ½ medium lemon
2½ tablespoons cornstarch

Optional
1 tablespoon heavy cream
1 tablespoon turbinado or sanding sugar

Preheat the oven to 400°F.

In a medium-size bowl, combine the pulp, sugar, salt, lemon juice, and cornstarch, and mix well. Set aside.

On a well-floured surface, roll out one portion of the dough until it is about ⅛-inch thick and will fit a 9-inch pie plate. Gently pick up the dough, center it over the pie plate, and ease it into the plate. Let the excess dough hang over the rim of the plate. Pour in the filling, shaking the pie plate to spread it out evenly.

Roll out the second portion of dough to the same size. Lay the dough over the filling. Trim the edges of both layers of dough to leave a 1-inch overhang. Pressing the edges together, fold them under and then decoratively crimp the perimeter. With a sharp knife, cut 5 vents in the top crust.

Bake the pie for 40 to 45 minutes, or until the top is golden brown. Let the pie cool to room temperature before enjoying.

Optional:
For a lovely sheen on the baked pie, use a pastry brush to paint the surface with the cream. If you like, sprinkle the sugar over the cream. As the pie bakes, the sugar will caramelize, and it will crackle when you slice a wedge of the freshly baked pie.

PINCH A LITTLE, TASTE A LOT

Most of the bakers I met in Naples get some help in what they call *pinching,* and judging from the thousands of pies these ladies produce, I can see why. A few steps are needed to achieve a delicious purple pie.

1. First, de-stem the grapes. Discard the stems. (Five cups of grapes will yield 2½ cups of prepared grape pulp.)

2. With the stem end facing out, gently pinch each grape, letting the seedy green pulp pop out into a bowl. Put the skins in another bowl. (You'll add the skins back to the pulp later. It's the skins that make the filling that deep, dark purple.)

3. When all the grapes have been pinched, it's time to cook the pulp. In a medium-size saucepan, bring the pulp to a boil over high heat. Lower the heat just slightly, and cook the pulp at a rolling boil for 5 minutes. At this point, the pulp should have released its seeds, turning into a seedy mush.

4. Strain the pulp through a fine-mesh sieve into a bowl. Use a spoon to push any grape solids through the mesh, leaving the seeds behind. Discard the seeds. You should have a viscous greenish liquid in the bowl. (Sounds attractive, doesn't it?)

5. Add the skins to the cooked pulp, and let the mixture come to room temperature. At first the mixture will appear grayish and unappetizing, but don't worry. The tannins and pectin in the skins will activate as the mixture sits, softening the skins and turning the pulp rosy. (When baked, the mixture will turn a deep purple.)

6. When the pulp is ready, you can use it immediately for filling, refrigerate it for a few days, or freeze it for up to several months.

Dutch Apple Sack Pie

They grow a lot of apples in the Northeast, and therefore they bake quite a lot of apple pies. Countless cookbooks tout apple pie recipes that claim to be the most delicious, the most flavorful, or the most time-tested—but this is the most unusual recipe that I have come across. It is a single-crusted pie with a streusel topping—both features of a typical Dutch-style apple pie. Sounds rather unremarkable, right? But it's not what goes into this pie that makes it exceptional—it's how you bake it. Once you've assembled the pie, you place it in a brown paper bag— a regular old grocery store bag does the trick—and seal it. The pie steams as it bakes, and the end result is fruit that is oh-so-tender. If you grew up in a house that was anything like mine, your parents probably kept a pile of brown paper grocery bags stacked under the kitchen sink or in a kitchen cupboard. I only wish that I had known about this pie when I was younger. Life would have been sweeter.

½ recipe Standard Pie Dough (page 28)

For the filling

4 large baking apples, such as Granny Smith or
    Pippin, peeled, cored, and cut into ¼-inch slices
    (approximately 5 cups)

½ cup sugar

½ teaspoon ground cinnamon

Juice of ½ medium lemon

2 tablespoons all-purpose flour

1 tablespoon cornstarch

For the streusel topping
½ cup brown sugar
½ cup all-purpose flour
½ teaspoon ground cinnamon
Pinch of kosher salt
8 tablespoons (1 stick) unsalted butter, cut into
    ½-inch cubes, at room temperature

Preheat the oven to 425°F.

On a well-floured surface, roll out the dough until it is about ⅛-inch thick and will fit a 9-inch pie plate. Gently pick up the dough, center it over the pie plate, and ease it into the plate. Trim the edges of the dough to leave a 1-inch overhang. Fold the edges under, and then decoratively crimp the perimeter. Return the pie shell to the refrigerator to chill until the filling is ready.

Make the filling: In a large bowl, toss the apples with the sugar and the cinnamon. Pour in the lemon juice, and toss again. Add the flour and the cornstarch, tossing to coat the apples. Set aside.

Make the streusel: In a small bowl, mix the brown sugar, flour, cinnamon, and salt until blended. Add the butter, and use your fingers to work the butter into the mixture until it forms pea-size lumps. Set aside.

Remove the pie shell from the refrigerator, and pour the apple filling into it, shaking the pie plate to spread it out evenly. Pat the streusel topping onto the surface, covering the apples evenly.

Take a large brown paper bag, place the pie inside the bag,

and fold the end of the bag over twice to close the opening. To secure it, staple or paper-clip the opening. Place the bag on a baking sheet and bake the pie for 45 minutes.

Remove the bagged pie from the oven. Carefully cut open the bag and remove the pie. Discard the bag, and return the pie to the baking sheet. Continue to bake for another 10 to 15 minutes, or until the streusel is golden brown. Remove the pie from the oven, and let it cool to room temperature before enjoying.

Note:

Early on as the pie bakes, your kitchen will smell like paper. Don't worry—the scent of spiced apples will soon overtake the space.

Crunchy Cranberry Pie

Before I moved to New England, I thought of cranberries as synonymous with Thanksgiving. My only experience of the cranberry came when my parents plopped a can of cranberry sauce, either jellied or chunky, into a bowl and set it on the Thanksgiving table. I saw the fruit strictly as a tart accompaniment to a slice of turkey. Maybe it was the crispness in the air come autumn, or the crunch of fallen leaves under my feet, or my palate finally maturing, but as soon as I moved to Connecticut, I was roused from my cranberry slumber.

I still eat them in sauce form at Thanksgiving, but now I find myself adding cranberries to braised meat dishes, mixing them into scones, and, of course, baking them into sweet-tart pies. In this pie, the whole berries, juicy and ready to burst, pop in the mouth as you bite into them. A baking apple and a bit of pure maple syrup balance the berries' natural acidity, and a buttery oatmeal-pecan streusel tops the pie—hence the "crunchy" in the name.

½ recipe Standard Pie Dough (page 28) or
  Whole Wheat Pie Dough (page 40)

For the filling
2½ cups cranberries, washed and patted dry
1 medium baking apple, such as Granny Smith,
  peeled, cored, and diced into ½-inch cubes (1½ cups)
⅓ cup pure maple syrup

⅓ cup sugar

Pinch of kosher salt

½ teaspoon almond extract

2 tablespoons all-purpose flour

For the streusel topping

½ cup all-purpose flour

¼ cup rolled oats

½ cup chopped pecans

½ cup brown sugar

½ teaspoon ground cinnamon

Pinch of kosher salt

6 tablespoons (¾ stick) unsalted butter, chilled,
  cut into ½-inch cubes

Preheat the oven to 375°F.

On a well-floured surface, roll out the dough until it is about ⅛-inch thick and will fit a 9-inch pie plate. Gently pick up the dough, center it over the pie plate, and ease it into the plate. Trim the edges of the dough to leave a 1-inch overhang. Fold the edges under, and then decoratively crimp the perimeter. Return the pie shell to the refrigerator to chill until the filling is ready.

Make the filling: In a medium-size bowl, combine the cranberries, apple, maple syrup, and sugar, and toss gently to coat. Add the salt and almond extract, and toss again. Add the flour and toss gently to coat.

Make the streusel: In another medium-size bowl, combine the flour, oats, pecans, brown sugar, cinnamon, and salt, and toss to mix. Add the butter, and use your fingers to work the butter into the dry mixture until the topping resembles large, coarse crumbs.

Remove the pie shell from the refrigerator, and pour the filling into it, shaking the pie plate gently to distribute it evenly. Pat the streusel topping evenly onto the surface, covering the cranberry filling.

Bake the pie for 50 to 55 minutes, or until the streusel is golden brown and juices are bubbling up through the surface. Remove the pie from the oven, and let it cool to room temperature before enjoying.

Cheddar-Crusted Apple Pie

Many New Englanders believe that the only way to eat apple pie is with a thick slice of cheddar cheese, either melted right on top or served on the side. They'll swear to you that it is the ultimate salty-sweet combination, a combination gaining ever more currency in the dessert world (just look at the rage for salted caramels). Well, New Englanders are right—apple pie is delicious with cheddar cheese. But rather than dictate how your guests should eat their pie, you can pull a sneak attack and mix the cheddar right into the crust. I once served this pie as the culmination to a fall meal, and after taking his first bite, one of the guests exclaimed, "The crust is like the best cheese cracker ever!" I took that as a compliment.

For the crust
2 cups all-purpose flour
⅓ cup finely ground cornmeal
2 tablespoons sugar
½ teaspoon kosher salt
8 tablespoons (1 stick) unsalted butter, chilled, cut into ½-inch pieces
6 tablespoons vegetable shortening, chilled, cut into ½-inch pieces
4 ounces white cheddar cheese, grated, (approximately 1½ cups)
2 large egg yolks
⅓ cup ice water, plus more if needed

For the filling

Approximately 5 tart baking apples, such as
  Granny Smith or Pippin, peeled, cored, and cut
  into ¼-inch slices (6 cups)

¼ cup plus 2 tablespoons sugar

¼ cup brown sugar

1 tablespoon fresh lemon juice

½ teaspoon ground cinnamon

¼ teaspoon ground nutmeg, preferably freshly grated
  (see page 155)

Pinch of kosher salt

2 tablespoons all-purpose flour

2 tablespoons unsalted butter, cut into ½-inch cubes

Make the crust: The addition of cheese makes the use of a food processor necessary. Combine the flour, cornmeal, sugar, and salt in the bowl of a food processor. Pulse briefly to mix. Add the butter and shortening and pulse until the mixture resembles a coarse meal. Add the cheese and pulse until just combined (the mixture will not come together yet). Transfer the mixture to a medium-size mixing bowl.

In a small bowl, beat the egg yolks with the ⅓ cup of ice water. Pour this into the flour mixture, and with your hands, work the mixture until it forms a shaggy mass of dough (add more ice water, 1 tablespoon at a time, if needed). When the dough comes together, divide it in half, flatten both halves into disks, and wrap them in plastic wrap. Refrigerate for at least 1 hour, or as long as 2 days.

When you are ready to make the pie, preheat the oven to 425°F.

Make the filling: Combine the apples, sugars, and lemon juice in a large bowl, and toss to mix. Add the cinnamon, nutmeg, and salt, tossing to mix. Add the flour and toss gently to coat the fruit.

On a well-floured surface, roll out one portion of the dough until it is about ⅛-inch thick and will fit a 9-inch pie plate. Gently pick up the dough, center it over the pie plate, and ease it into the plate. Let the excess dough hang over the rim of the plate. Pour in the filling, and shake the pie plate gently to distribute the fruit evenly. Dot the surface of the filling with the butter.

Roll out the second portion of dough to the same size. Lay the dough over the filling. Trim the edges of both layers of dough to leave a 1-inch overhang. Pressing the edges together, fold them under, and then decoratively crimp the perimeter. With a sharp knife, cut 5 vents in the top crust.

Place the pie on a baking sheet and bake for 10 minutes. Then reduce the heat to 375° and continue to bake for another 50 to 55 minutes, until the crust is golden brown and speckled with cheese. (If the crust begins to brown too quickly, tent it with a piece of aluminum foil.) Remove the pie from the oven, and let it cool to room temperature before enjoying.

Pumpkin Pie

The saying should be "as American as pumpkin pie," because while apples are thought to have originated as far east as China, it is the pumpkin that is indigenous to North America. Native Americans used dried pumpkin as a jerky-like substance to snack on throughout the long winters, as well as cutting and drying strips of pumpkin and weaving them into mats. When the first European settlers came to the New World, they too began to cook and bake with this new crop. They found pumpkins texturally similar to the winter squashes they had been cooking in Europe, so they baked, boiled, mashed, and flavored the pumpkin. Recipes for winter squash pie were developed into pumpkin pie—and a favorite of holiday tables was born!

This recipe uses freshly roasted sugar pumpkin pulp, but you can use commercially canned pumpkin purée, if you must. Making your own pumpkin purée could not be any simpler, and it makes for a rich and supremely smooth filling. It also freezes beautifully, so you could roast a few sugar pumpkins at the beginning of the season and eat pumpkin pie all year long!

½ recipe Standard Pie Dough (page 28) or
   Sour Cream Pie Dough (page 36)

1¼ cups pumpkin purée, preferably homemade
   (see page 75)
½ cup sugar

¼ cup brown sugar
½ teaspoon kosher salt
½ teaspoon ground ginger
1 teaspoon ground cinnamon
1 tablespoon all-purpose flour
2 large eggs
½ cup heavy cream
½ cup whole milk
½ teaspoon vanilla extract

Preheat the oven to 400°F.

On a well-floured surface, roll out the dough until it is about ⅛-inch thick and will fit a 9-inch pie plate. Gently pick up the dough, center it over the pie plate, and ease the dough into the plate. Trim the edges of the dough to leave a 1-inch overhang. Fold the edges under, and then decoratively crimp the perimeter. Return the pie shell to the refrigerator to chill until the filling is ready.

In a medium-size bowl, combine the pumpkin, sugars, salt, ginger, cinnamon, and flour, and stir to mix.

In a small bowl, combine the eggs, cream, milk, and vanilla, and beat lightly to mix. Pour the egg mixture into the pumpkin mixture, stirring to blend.

Remove the pie shell from the refrigerator, and pour the filling into the shell.

Bake the pie for 50 to 55 minutes, or until the filling is almost set. The center should still look slightly undercooked—the residual heat of

Note:
One 3-pound
pumpkin yields
approximately
1½ cups of purée.

the pie will continue to cook the filling after you've removed it from the oven. (If the crust browns too quickly during baking, tent the pie with a piece of aluminum foil for the duration of the cooking time.) Remove the pie from the oven, and let it cool to room temperature before enjoying.

HOW TO MAKE HOMEMADE PUMPKIN PURÉE

No, pumpkins don't grow in cans, and yes, it is easy to make your own pumpkin purée. Homemade pumpkin purée is lighter, smoother, and more delicate than canned purée. It takes only about an hour to roast a sugar pumpkin, the variety used for baking (sometimes called "pie pumpkins" and not to be confused with the standard jack-o'-lantern pumpkins left over from Halloween), and that time is largely unattended. No stirring, no tenting with foil, no brushing with olive oil. The most work that you'll have to do is scraping out the pumpkin's webby pulp. Once you've done that, there's a bonus: you can pan-roast the seeds and snack on them while the pumpkin is in the oven. After you've roasted and puréed the pumpkin, it'll need to drain overnight (watery purée equals soggy pie), but again, just stick it in the refrigerator and ignore.

One 3- to 5-pound sugar pumpkin

Preheat the oven to 375°F.

Using a sharp knife, cut off and discard the stem end of the pumpkin. Slice the pumpkin in half through the stem end. Scrape the seeds and pulp out of the interior. Place the pumpkin halves cut side down on a baking sheet, and bake for 45 to 70 minutes, depending on size. The pumpkin is ready when you can poke it easily with a fork. Remove the pumpkin halves from the oven and let them cool slightly.

Scrape out the pumpkin's flesh, and discard the skin. Place the flesh in a food processor and process it until completely smooth. This should take about 1 minute.

Put the puréed pumpkin flesh in a cheesecloth-lined colander or sieve, and place the colander over a bowl. Refrigerate overnight. By morning the puréed pumpkin will have exuded up to a cup of liquid, which you should discard.

Sealed in an airtight container, the strained purée will keep in the refrigerator for a few days or in the freezer for a few months.

Honey Pie

My husband and I had been living in New Haven just over a year when I first met Vincent Kay. In my head, I like to think of Vincent as "Vincent Kay, Man of the Northeast." He does a bit of everything: trains dogs, leads hunting expeditions, butchers game, keeps chickens, grows the most beautiful, plump garlic that you will ever cook with, and is an apiarist to boot. Vincent has his own cottage industry producing local artisanal honey. When his bees are not busy pollinating orchards all around the state on a for-hire basis, he keeps them in various rural (and not so rural) locations. They feed off local wild plants and trees, and Vincent augments their diet by mixing up thousands of pounds of his own sugar solution. Vincent's bees are happy bees. They produce gorgeous golden-red honey, not to mention amber wax for beeswax candles. Needless to say, my life in food has been greatly influenced by Vincent's generosity. It would have been impossible for me to write this book without including a recipe honoring Vincent and his bees.

In essence, this is a custard pie starring honey in the featured role. The flavor of the pie depends in large part on the sort of honey used. The bees around New Haven produce a particularly caramel-scented nectar—some say that my pie tastes a bit like flan. Whether or not you call a beekeeper friend, try to use a local honey, and think of Vincent as you enjoy this pie.

½ recipe Standard Pie Dough (page 28) or Leaf Lard
  Pie Dough (page 32)

¾ cup honey

¼ cup sour cream

4 large eggs

1 teaspoon vanilla extract

Pinch of ground nutmeg, preferably freshly grated (see page 155)

½ teaspoon ground ginger

Pinch of kosher salt

Preheat the oven to 375°F.

On a well-floured surface, roll out the dough until it is about ⅛-inch thick and will fit a 9-inch pie plate. Gently pick up the dough, center it over the pie plate, and ease it into the plate. Trim the edges of the dough to leave a 1-inch overhang. Fold the edges under, and then decoratively crimp the perimeter. Return the pie shell to the refrigerator to chill until the filling is ready.

In a small saucepan over medium heat, warm the honey until it is completely fluid. Once heated, the honey should have the consistency of heavy cream. Set aside.

In a medium-size bowl, combine the sour cream, eggs, vanilla, nutmeg, ginger, and salt, and whisk to blend. Add the warm honey, and whisk until thoroughly incorporated.

Remove the pie shell from the refrigerator, and pour the filling into the shell. Bake the pie for approximately 40 minutes, or until the filling is set. (If the crust browns too quickly while baking, tent the pie with a piece of aluminum foil.) The filling will puff substantially while baking, but will collapse once you remove the pie from the oven. Let the pie cool to room temperature before enjoying.

Bakewell Pie

Bakewell tart is an English dessert—still popular today—with a long pedigree. The perfect not-too-sweet treat for afternoon tea, it's an almond sponge cake layered with raspberry jam. In the great history of Americans borrowing from other cultures, the transformation of Bakewell tart into pie has to be one of the happier adaptations. While this pie is an English transplant and could come from any one of the American colonies, its first mention is in the 1886 "receipt" book The Unrivalled Cook-book and Housekeeper's Guide, *edited by the pseudonymous "Mrs. Washington" and published in New York City. Heirloom Bakewell pie recipes call for ratafia, a cordial made from the pits of cherries or peaches, or from bitter almonds. Instead of using this cordial, which is somewhat difficult to find, I use ground blanched almonds, which play off the raspberry jam beautifully. Try this pie, and don't forget to thank Mrs. Washington, whoever she—or he, for that matter—may have been!*

½ recipe Standard Pie Dough (page 28) or Rich and
Buttery Pie Dough (page 30)

½ cup raspberry jam
8 tablespoons (1 stick) unsalted butter, melted
½ cup sugar
½ cup ground blanched almonds or almond meal
3 large eggs
¼ cup all-purpose flour

½ teaspoon kosher salt

½ teaspoon almond extract

Preheat the oven to 375°F.

On a well-floured surface, roll out the dough until it is about ⅛-inch thick and will fit a 9-inch pie plate. Gently pick up the dough, center it over the pie plate, and ease it into the plate. Trim the edges of the dough to leave a 1-inch overhang. Fold the edges under, and then decoratively crimp the perimeter. Spread the jam evenly over the bottom of the pie shell. Place the jam-lined shell in the refrigerator to chill while you prepare the sponge filling.

Using an electric mixer, mix the melted butter and the sugar in a medium-size bowl until blended into a pastelike consistency. Alternating, add the ground almonds and the eggs (one at a time) to the bowl, incorporating each before adding the next, and ending with an egg. Sift in the flour and salt, and beat until smooth. Fold in the almond extract.

Remove the jam-lined pie shell from the refrigerator, and pour the almond sponge mixture into it. Carefully place the pie in the oven. Bake for approximately 35 minutes, or until the crust and the surface of the pie are golden brown. Let cool for at least 1 hour before serving.

Chipmunk Pie

I'll admit it: the first thing that charmed me about this pie was its name. I came across it in The Delaware Heritage Cookbook, *a 1987 cookbook compiled to commemorate the 200th anniversary of Delaware's state ratification. In essence, the book reads like a spiral-bound community cookbook, except that the community in question is the entire state of Delaware. The origins of the recipes that fill these types of cookbooks can be hard to pin down. Some are family recipes, others—usually highly era-specific—came from the back of food boxes, while others still were the innovations of creative home cooks. Mrs. Celia Miller of Farmington donated the recipe for chipmunk pie. Her introductory note reads, "This unique dessert is served often at our covered dish dinners at Bethany Church of the Brethren." That is a covered dish dinner to which I would like to be invited.*

½ recipe Standard Pie Dough (page 28)

2 large eggs
½ cup sugar
½ cup brown sugar
½ cup all-purpose flour
1 teaspoon baking powder
½ teaspoon vanilla extract
Pinch of kosher salt
1 medium baking apple, such as Granny Smith or
    Pippin, peeled, cored, and diced into ½-inch cubes
    (1½ cups)

½ cup roughly chopped nuts (pecans, walnuts,
hazelnuts, etc.), one variety or mixed

Preheat the oven to 350°F.

On a well-floured surface, roll out the dough until it is about ⅛-inch thick and will fit a 9-inch pie plate. Gently pick up the dough, center it over the pie plate, and ease it into the plate. Trim the edges of the dough to leave a 1-inch overhang. Fold the edges under, and then decoratively crimp the perimeter. Return the pie shell to the refrigerator to chill until the filling is ready.

In a medium-size bowl, beat the eggs. Add the sugars and flour, and stir thoroughly to incorporate the dry ingredients. Add the baking powder, vanilla, and salt, and continue to stir. Add the apple pieces and the nuts, and fold them into the mixture.

Remove the pie shell from the refrigerator, and pour the filling into the shell. Bake for 40 to 45 minutes, or until the surface of the pie is golden brown and crisp. The filling will puff, almost like a macaron, while baking, and then deflate. Let the pie cool to room temperature before enjoying.

Shoofly Pie

The moment I began working on this book, I knew that shoofly pie would have a place on the list—not so much for personal reasons, but because shoofly pie is a Pennsylvania Dutch standard. In fact, whenever the book came up in conversation, often one of the first things people wanted to know was whether I was going to include shoofly pie. I would nod and ask if they happened to have a favorite recipe for the pie. Each time I did, my question was met with the same response: "Oh, I've never actually had *the pie; I just know that it's a regional specialty." And so my quest began.*

The pie is traditionally made with lots of molasses, and it's thought that the name derives from the need to wave one's hand above it, shooing away syrup-loving flies. This tells you that the Pennsylvania Dutch liked their desserts sweet! There are as many variations on shoofly pie as there are syrup-hungry flies, but the two main types are "wet bottom" and "dry bottom." In a wet-bottom pie, the layer closest to the bottom crust is a smooth molasses-egg custard, with a crumb top. A dry-bottom pie alternates layers of crumb topping with a similar molasses filling, which gives the pie a firm, almost cakey crumb. But no matter the style—wet or dry—the mainstay of the pie is molasses. During the settlement of America, the settlers often found their cupboards close to bare during the winter and early spring. What was left in the larder were pantry staples—flour, lard, and molasses—and this dessert was born.

After trying quite a few shoofly pies, I came to appreciate the chewiness of the dry-bottom version—and that's what this one is. Molasses can be an acquired taste, so I use a light hand with it here. I find a bit of ginger and cinnamon lend the pie a gingerbreadlike flavor. This shoofly pie is not too sweet, and it makes a good break-fast pie served with a dollop of plain or vanilla yogurt.

½ recipe Standard Pie Dough (page 28) or Whole
   Wheat Pie Dough (page 40)

For the crumb topping
1 cup all-purpose flour
½ cup dark brown sugar
½ teaspoon ground cinnamon
¼ teaspoon ground ginger
⅛ teaspoon ground nutmeg, preferably freshly grated
   (see page 155)
Pinch of kosher salt
5 tablespoons unsalted butter, chilled,
   chopped into ½-inch cubes

For the molasses filling
½ cup unsulfured molasses
2 large eggs
½ cup boiling water
½ teaspoon baking soda

Preheat the oven to 375°F.

On a well-floured surface, roll out the dough until it is about ⅛-inch thick and will fit a 9-inch pie plate. Gently pick up the dough, center it over the pie plate, and ease it into the plate. Trim the edges of the dough to leave a 1-inch overhang. Fold the edges under, and then decoratively crimp the perimeter. Return the pie shell to the refrigerator to chill until the filling is ready.

Make the crumb topping: In a medium-size bowl, combine the flour, brown sugar, cinnamon, ginger, nutmeg, and salt, and mix thoroughly. Add the butter, and work it into the dry ingredients with your hands, creating a rough mixture. Continue working the butter into the dry ingredients until the topping resembles large, coarse crumbs.

Remove the pie shell from the refrigerator. Sprinkle about half of the crumb mixture into the pie shell, and shake the pie plate gently to distribute it evenly. Set aside.

Make the molasses filling: In a medium-size bowl, combine the molasses and the eggs and beat until smooth.

In a small bowl, combine the boiling water and the baking soda, stirring to dissolve the soda. All at once, add the water mixture to the molasses mixture (the mixture will bubble up), and beat well until combined—it's crucial to work quickly to prevent the mixture from bubbling over.

Pour the molasses filling over the crumb layer in the pie shell. Sprinkle the remainder of the crumb topping over the surface of the pie, creating a ring of topping around the perimeter of the pie and leaving the center of the pie nearly open. (This allows the filling to expand, if necessary.)

Bake the pie for 35 to 40 minutes. The molasses filling will bubble up, but will firm as the pie cools. This pie may be eaten when still a bit warm.

Maple-Walnut Pie

This pie hails from Vermont, where maple syrup is king. (Vermont is the largest producer of pure maple syrup in the United States.) In early spring, temperatures in Vermont alternate between thawing and freezing. This fluctuation encourages the sugar-laden sap of maple trees to flow. Syrup makers collect the sap from the trees by drilling small, shallow holes into their trunks. They boil the sap in sugarhouses, evaporating gallons of water from the sap and making the concentrated syrup.

A quick glance at the ingredients list might give you the impression that this pie is similar to pecan pie, but it's not. Pecan pie is made with corn syrup, which has a rather neutral sweet flavor. This pie is baked with woodsy maple syrup. The flavor is reminiscent of the perfect Sunday morning breakfast, with maple syrup cascading down a short stack of pancakes.

Compounding the delicious breakfast parallel, I have added some coffee granules to the filling. As lovely as the maple taste is, it is very assertive in its sweetness. The coffee doesn't lend its flavor to the pie; it just reduces the intensity of the maple syrup. The walnuts, which also balance the sweetness with a pleasing bitterness, rise to the top during baking. The sugar in the syrup almost caramelizes the nuts, creating a shatteringly crisp top. If you like, garnish each slice with a bit of unsweetened whipped cream.

½ recipe Whole Wheat Pie Dough (page 40)

3 large eggs
1 cup pure maple syrup (see Note)
¼ cup brown sugar
2 tablespoons unsalted butter, melted
2 tablespoons all-purpose flour
1 teaspoon instant coffee granules
¼ teaspoon kosher salt
1 teaspoon vanilla extract
½ cup coarsely chopped walnuts

Note:

There are several grades of maple syrup: fancy (the mildest), medium amber, dark amber, and grade B (the richest and most full-bodied). For this recipe you should use either dark amber or grade B maple syrup. You want to taste the buttery maple flavor. Never *use the imitation syrup; the pie just will not be the same!*

Preheat the oven to 375°F.

On a well-floured surface, roll out the dough until it is about ⅛-inch thick and will fit a 9-inch pie plate. Gently pick up the dough, center it over the pie plate, and ease it into the plate. Trim the edges of the dough to leave a 1-inch overhang. Fold the edges under, and then decoratively crimp the perimeter. Return the pie shell to the refrigerator to chill until the filling is ready.

In a medium-size bowl, beat the eggs until frothy. Add the maple syrup and brown sugar, and whisk until well combined. Add the melted butter, flour, coffee granules, salt, and vanilla, and continue to whisk until all the ingredients are blended. Fold in the walnuts.

Remove the pie shell from the refrigerator, and pour the filling into the shell. Bake the pie for 40 to 45 minutes, or until the filling is set. The filling may puff substantially as it bakes, but it will fall as it cools. Let the pie cool to room temperature before enjoying.

Homemade Mincemeat Pie

Traditional mincemeat is a dark, sweet paste made of dried fruit, warm spices, oftentimes brandy or some other type of liquor, and meat—either beef, venison, or, at the very least, beef suet, the type of fat typically found around the loins and kidneys of a cow. Mincemeat is an old food—early recipes date to the late Middle Ages, when cooking meat in spirits was a useful method of preserving. English settlers brought mincemeat to the American colonies, and though it was still popular through the early twentieth century, few Americans eat real mincemeat today, and even fewer make it themselves. You might find jarred mincemeat in the baking aisle of a supermarket—it's usually lurking on a bottom shelf next to the canned cherry and apple pie filling. See that jar of deep brown filling? The one that looks like lumpy gravy? That's the stuff I'm talking about. Mincemeat is a lot like fruitcake—great when homemade, but the store-bought variety leaves much to be desired. My recipe makes a delicious traditional-tasting mincemeat while maintaining a meatless list of ingredients, and will have each of your diners asking for another slice.

    1 recipe Standard Pie Dough (page 28) or
      Sour Cream Pie Dough (page 36)

    One 8-ounce jar homemade mincemeat (recipe follows)

    Optional
    1 tablespoon heavy cream
    1 tablespoon turbinado or sanding sugar

87

Optional:
For a lovely sheen on the baked pie, use a pastry brush to paint the surface with the cream. If you like, sprinkle the sugar over the cream. As the pie bakes, the sugar will caramelize, and it will crackle when you slice a wedge of the freshly baked pie.

Preheat the oven to 425°F.

On a well-floured surface, roll out one portion of the dough until it is about ⅛-inch thick and will fit a 9-inch pie plate. Gently pick up the dough, center it over the pie plate, and ease it into the plate. Let the excess dough hang over the rim. Pour in the mincemeat filling, and spread it out evenly.

Roll out the second portion of dough to the same size. Lay the dough over the filling, and trim the edges of both layers of dough to leave a 1-inch overhang. Press the edges together, fold them, and then decoratively crimp the perimeter. With a sharp knife, cut 5 vents in the top crust.

Bake the pie for 15 minutes. Then reduce the heat to 375° and continue to bake for another 25 to 30 minutes, until the crust is golden brown. Let the pie cool to room temperature before enjoying.

Mincemeat

My mincemeat recipe is meat-free; creamy butter takes the place of suet. The list of ingredients looks long, but don't let that put you off. Except for chopping and peeling the apples, it's simple to put together. To me, mincemeat tastes like the holidays. Moist, chewy, and dense, simmered until the dried fruit reconstitutes, this mincemeat could become a new family tradition.

Makes four 8-ounce jars (filling for 4 pies)

12 tablespoons (1½ sticks) unsalted butter
4 pounds mixed tart apples, cored, peeled, and diced
1 cup dried cranberries

1 cup golden raisins

1 cup dark raisins

1 cup dried currants

⅔ cup chopped pecans

1 cup dark brown sugar

½ cup unsulfured molasses

½ cup apple juice

½ cup brandy

*¼ teaspoon ground nutmeg, preferably freshly grated
    (see page 155)*

1½ teaspoons ground cinnamon

½ teaspoon ground allspice

½ teaspoon ground cloves

1 teaspoon ground ginger

1 teaspoon kosher salt

2 teaspoons grated orange zest

2 teaspoons grated lemon zest

Juice of 1 medium orange

Juice of 1 medium lemon

For canning (optional)
Four 8-ounce jars, with lids and sealing rings

Melt the butter in a large pot over medium heat. Add the apples, and stir well to coat them completely in the butter. Add all the remaining ingredients to the pot. (It doesn't matter what order you add them in, or how quickly; the mixture will be simmering for quite a while.) Give everything a good stir, and bring the mixture to a boil over medium heat. When it reaches a boil, reduce the heat to low and simmer, stirring occasionally, for 45 minutes. By this stage, the mixture will have

Note:

This project takes a while, so it's best to make the mincemeat in advance. I find it easiest to prepare the mincemeat pre-holiday, around October. Apples are at their peak then, and the storage time gives the mincemeat a chance for all its flavors to meld—plus it's all done before the holiday madness. The recipe yields four 8-ounce jars of mincemeat, enough for four pies. In the past, I have kept two jars for myself, just enough to get through the holidays. The other two jars I give to like-minded friends with a penchant for old-timey desserts. And don't worry, canning the mincemeat is really simple! Once canned, the jars will hold for up to 1 year in your larder.

reached a jammy consistency. The apples should have broken down, the various dried fruits should be indistinguishable, and the whole mixture should be a dark brownish color.

Remove the pot from the heat. If you will be storing the mincemeat for up to 1 month, divide the contents among four clean 8-ounce jars, and store them in the refrigerator. If you prefer to can the mincemeat for longer storage, follow the instructions below.

To can the mincemeat: First sterilize the empty jars and their lids and sealing rings by submerging them in boiling water for 10 minutes. With kitchen tongs, carefully remove the jars from the water. Fill each sterilized jar with mincemeat, leaving ½ inch of headspace at the top. Gently knock the filled jars on the counter to release any air bubbles. If necessary, clean the outside of each jar. Screw on the lids and sealing rings. Place the jars in a large pot of water, with enough liquid to cover them by 1 inch. (You can use the same water you used for sterilizing the jars.) Bring the water to a boil, and heat the jars at a constant simmer for 25 minutes. Turn off the heat and let the jars rest, submerged in the water, for 5 minutes. Then remove the jars from the water bath and let them cool to room temperature. The canned mincemeat will keep for up to 1 year in a cool dark place.

Maine Blueberry Pie

The Maine blueberry is one of those berries that seems too good to be true. It is not simply an ordinary blueberry grown in the state of Maine. It is wild. Often referred to as low-bush berries, Maine blueberries grow on bushes that creep, feet from the ground, and bloom in two-year cycles, producing berries only every other year. The farmers of Maine tend to the bushes during their dormant years, ensuring a healthy bush during fruit-bearing years. The sweet-tart flavor of a Maine wild blueberry is like a blueberry that has been training for a marathon. It is smaller, and more flavorful and intense, than the cultivated variety.

This is a pie that is supremely blue—and I do mean the color. It's simply overflowing with delicious beads of blueberries. Even if you think you don't love blueberries, after one taste of this pie you won't be able to deny that it is delicious—and you will probably finish that slice with a happy smile.

If you don't live in Maine—and since this state has one of the smallest populations of any in the country, you probably do not—feel free to make this pie with regular blueberries. This pie is assertive and fresh, flavored simply with a bit of lemon juice and a touch of vanilla.

1 recipe Standard Pie Dough (page 28) or Cornmeal
   Pie Dough (page 38)

5 cups blueberries, preferably Maine wild blueberries,
   washed

¾ cup sugar

2 tablespoons all-purpose flour

1 tablespoon cornstarch

Juice of 1 medium lemon

1 teaspoon vanilla extract

Pinch of kosher salt

Optional

1 tablespoon heavy cream

1 tablespoon turbinado or sanding sugar

Preheat the oven to 425°F.

In a medium-size bowl, combine the blueberries, sugar, flour, cornstarch, lemon juice, vanilla, and salt. Toss well but gently, keeping the berries intact. Set aside.

On a well-floured surface, roll out one portion of the dough until it is about ⅛-inch thick and will fit a 9-inch pie plate. Gently pick up the dough, center it over the pie plate, and ease it into the plate. Let the excess dough hang over the rim. Pour in the filling, and spread it out evenly.

Roll out the second portion of dough to the same size. Lay the dough over the filling, and trim the edges of both layers of dough to leave a 1-inch overhang. Pressing the edges together, fold them under, and then decoratively crimp the perimeter. With a sharp knife, cut 5 vents in the top crust.

Bake the pie for 15 minutes. Then reduce the heat to 375° and continue to bake for another 35 to 40 minutes, until the crust is golden brown. Let the pie cool to room temperature before enjoying.

Optional:
For a lovely sheen on the baked pie, use a pastry brush to paint the surface with the cream. If you like, sprinkle the sugar over the cream. As the pie bakes, the sugar will caramelize, and it will crackle when you slice a wedge of the freshly baked pie.

PIES of the SOUTH

Americans have a long history of romanticizing Southern cuisine, from barbecue to Creole dishes such as jambalaya to soul food, perhaps the region's most emblematic style of cooking. Pie plays no little part in that reputation: pecan pie and sweet potato pie—two American classics—are practically synonymous with the South, and no dinner there would be complete without a slice, especially if guests are invited.

At the Texas Pie Kitchen in Austin, Jen Biddle merges the South's delicious history of pie making with its equally famous legacy of unparalleled hospitality. For the people who work at the Texas Pie Kitchen—a nonprofit job-training program —pie is so much more than a decadent dessert; it is a path to self-sufficiency and self-reliance, and a source of pride in hard work and a job well done.

It all started back in 2000, when Jen, a social work grad student and record store clerk at Austin's Waterloo Records, decided to make a pecan pie for one of her favorite artists, Lyle Lovett, who was coming to the shop for an in-store appearance. She used her grandma's dough recipe, and the recipe for the filling came from her aunt. The pie was a hit, and Mr. Lovett thanked her profusely. Later, when Willie Nelson was scheduled for an in-store appearance, her coworkers urged her to make another pie for the country music legend. Jen didn't play favorites, and obliged. Jen's fan base soon expanded from country music crooners to her coworkers and friends, and as her reputation grew, she began to take special orders and bake and sell pies from her home. With that, the Texas Pie Kitchen was born. Her tiny business was hardly lucrative, but she enjoyed the baking—plus, she had larger plans for the Kitchen.

As a graduate student in social work, Jen was exposed on a daily basis to the hardships of Austin's impoverished and underserved residents; nearly 20 percent of Austin's population lives at or below the poverty level, and the largest percentage of those people are between the ages of eighteen and twenty-four. With Jen's success baking pies for paying customers, she began to think about the larger picture. Maybe she could combine two of her loves—making pie and helping others—to make a difference for Austin's at-risk youth. It took some years to develop a business plan, establish nonprofit status, recruit volunteers, and grow awareness and interest in the Texas Pie Kitchen, but Jen managed, and the Texas Pie Kitchen became what it is today.

In its incarnation as a job-training program, the Kitchen runs a six-month course that teaches its student-bakers the fundamentals of baking and pastry making, and pairs them with mentors who not only offer encouragement but also teach them self-reliance. The Kitchen sells pies to local cafes, caters larger events, and fills special orders, all while developing the students' customer service and money handling skills.

The Austin Resource Center for the Homeless (ARCH), a large shelter and community center in downtown Austin, houses the Texas Pie Kitchen's kitchen. Austin's main drag, Sixth Street, which is lined with bars, live music venues, and tequila shacks, is just a few blocks away. You can only imagine the music and drunken patrons that pour out these doors on any weekend night. But on the quiet Friday afternoon I visit, Sixth Street is a ghost town. The doors of ARCH are locked, but inside, the building is alive with social workers, volunteers, homeless people, and those citizens who are down on their luck. I peer through the door, and a no-nonsense but friendly young woman shoves it open. It's Jen Biddle. "Adrienne?" she asks, offering her hand. "Let's go up to the kitchen." I follow her up through the massive center and into a sizable kitchen. It is spotlessly clean, its stainless-steel surfaces gleaming, but I don't see any rolling pins, any sacks of flour or sugar, not even a pie plate. Jen tells me it is Thursday mornings when this space becomes the Texas Pie Kitchen.

My visit turns out to be a discussion about pie, about community, and about Austin.

Jen introduces me to Larrick Martin, the first student to complete the program at the Kitchen and now ARCH's kitchen manager. An affable young man, he is eager to talk about the six-month training program. Larrick found his way to the Kitchen through Austin's Housing Authority, one of the programs that the Texas Pie Kitchen works with. The Housing Authority has similar goals of breaking the poverty cycle within the city, in its case by offering low-income citizens affordable housing.

Larrick needed a bit of assistance, and the Kitchen was the perfect vehicle for him. He had always been interested in cooking—his free time was spent watching the Food Network—but before he entered the program, he had never done any baking. Larrick now takes his job as kitchen manager seriously. As manager he is given the pie recipes first, and he diligently bakes them up before sharing the recipes with the Kitchen's students. "I don't let anyone else [make pies] until I try them out first," he tells me.

As we stand around a stainless-steel table, drinking glasses of ice water from institutional-grade plastic cups, the conversation soon turns to making dough—the bane of many a baker's existence. Jen shares her top-secret family recipe only with the participants of the program. I think about the camaraderie and the trust that this must establish between Jen and the members of the Kitchen, how the recipe is like a secret handshake. While learning the pie recipes is a task completed by each student individually, "pastry we try to do step by step," Jen tells me. "There's just so much to do, and so much can go wrong." But Jen must be doing something right in her teaching, because Larrick makes a point of telling me, "I know dough like the back of my hand."

Over half of all the pies made by the Texas Pie Kitchen come from recipes either dreamed up by Jen or passed down through her family. There is the Dr Pepper Pecan Pie, made with soda-fountain syrup, corn syrup, and pecans; the best-selling German Chocolate Pecan Pie; and one of Jen's favorites, Eva's Strawberry Chocolate Cream Cheese Swirl Pie, a concoction of strawberries, chocolate ganache, and cream cheese anchored by a graham cracker crust. Jen created the pie when she was pregnant with her daughter, Eva. "I just put together a bunch of stuff I liked," says Jen. Her easygoing attitude toward dreaming up pies is in stark contrast to the Kitchen's mission to economically empower low-income people in north central Austin through small-business development and mentoring projects.

Officially started in February 2009, the Texas Pie Kitchen is a relatively new nonprofit, but Jen is already planning for the future. She has planted blueberry bushes and apple trees in the backyard of her home, with the hopes that they will bear fruit in coming years. What could be better than a truly local fruit pie? "We would love to have a storefront in a place where it's needed," Jen tells me. "Then this would truly be a community-supported project."

As my time at the Kitchen comes to a close, I jokingly ask Larrick if learning how to make pie was life-changing. He quickly answers: "Pie *did* change my life. It kept me out of trouble." Looking around the pristine kitchen, successfully managed by Larrick, I nod, embarrassed by my own sarcasm. I realize that sometimes a pie is more than pie—it can be about self-reliance and education. Pie can be a symbol of a job well done. A place like the Texas Pie Kitchen is showing its students this every day.

German Chocolate Pecan Pie

German chocolate cake isn't German at all. In 1852, Sam German—an American—developed a sweet baking chocolate for Baker's Chocolate Company, and the company named the product after him: German's Chocolate Bar. Just over a century later, a Texas housewife sent the recipe for what she called "German's Chocolate Cake" to a Dallas newspaper. The recipe was a hit, and General Foods, which owned Baker's Chocolate, took notice and distributed the recipe to newspapers across the country. Over time, the possessive "s" in the cake's name was dropped. In this classic American cake, layers of rich chocolate cake alternate with gooey coconut and pecan filling.

Since the cake originated in Texas, it seems only fitting that the pie would come from there as well. With much the same ingredients as the cake—chocolate, pecans, and sweetened flaked coconut—this pie is hardly an exercise in restraint. Pecan pie lovers will adore this pie; for those with more ascetic tastes, I suggest cutting the chocolate chips down to half a cup. This pie is decadent; it is sweet; and it's definitely rich. It's clear why such a pie is one of the bestselling desserts that the Texas Pie Kitchen makes.

½ recipe Standard Pie Dough (page 28)

3 large eggs
1 cup sugar
3 tablespoons all-purpose flour

3 tablespoons unsalted butter, melted

1 cup dark corn syrup

1 tablespoon vanilla extract

Pinch of kosher salt

1 cup coarsely chopped pecans

1 cup semisweet chocolate chips, plus a handful for
   garnish

½ cup sweetened shredded coconut

Preheat the oven to 350°F.

On a well-floured surface, roll out the dough until it is about ⅛-inch thick and will fit a 9-inch pie plate. Gently pick up the dough, center it over the pie plate, and ease it into the plate. Trim the edges of the dough to leave a 1-inch overhang. Fold the edges under, and then decoratively crimp the perimeter. Return the pie shell to the refrigerator to chill until the filling is ready.

In a medium-size bowl, beat the eggs with a whisk. Add the sugar, flour, melted butter, corn syrup, vanilla, and salt, and continue to whisk until well combined. Fold in the chopped pecans, the cup of chocolate chips, and the coconut.

Remove the pie shell from the refrigerator, and pour the filling into the shell. Scatter the remaining chocolate chips over the filling. Bake the pie for 55 to 60 minutes, until the crust is golden brown and the filling is set. Remove the pie from the oven, and let it cool to room temperature before enjoying.

Key Lime Pie

This pie is the happy result of making do. Life in the Florida Keys is steamy and tropical—not the ideal climate for cows. So, long ago, before interstate highways and refrigerated shipping, Floridians had to rely on condensed milk because fresh milk was rarely available. Not exactly what most would want to top their morning cereal with, but it makes a mighty fine pie. Key limes, which were first introduced to Florida by Spanish colonists in the 1500s, grew throughout the Florida Keys until a hurricane destroyed many of the groves in 1926. Nowadays, when you find Key limes at the market, they more than likely come from Mexico.

To bake or not to bake? That is the question for true Key lime pie aficionados. When lime juice and condensed milk mix, a chemical reaction called souring occurs. Souring thickens the filling substantially, so baking is not required. But because the custard contains egg yolks, I briefly cook it in order to eliminate any hazard of food-borne illness (it also ensures a buoyant filling).

If you can't find Key limes at the market, go ahead and makes this pie anyway. It will still be delicious—even if it is only a lime pie!

1 Graham Cracker Crust (page 42)

For the filling
3 large egg yolks
One 14-ounce can sweetened condensed milk
Pinch of kosher salt
½ cup Key lime juice (from 10 to 12 Key limes)

2 teaspoons grated Key lime zest (from 6 to 8
   Key limes)

For the topping
¾ cup heavy cream
1 tablespoon confectioners' sugar

Preheat the oven to 350°F.

In the bowl of an electric mixer fitted with the whisk attachment, beat the egg yolks on high speed until fluffy, 2 to 3 minutes. With the mixer on medium speed, gradually add the condensed milk, and continue to beat until the mixture becomes pale and fluffy, 3 to 5 minutes. Scrape down the sides of the bowl. Then add the salt, lime juice, and lime zest, and beat for another 30 seconds or so, until well blended. The mixture will begin solidifying.

Pour the filling into the prepared crust, spreading it out evenly with an offset spatula. Bake the pie for 10 to 12 minutes, just until the filling is set and is beginning to develop a skin. Remove the pie from the oven and place it on a wire rack. Let the pie cool to room temperature. Then cover it carefully with plastic wrap, and refrigerate it until ready to serve. (The pie can be made up to a day in advance.)

Just before you're ready to serve the pie, combine the cream and the confectioners' sugar in a medium bowl, and using an electric mixer, whip until it forms soft peaks. Mound the whipped cream on the surface of the pie, creating a smooth layer. Serve chilled.

Southern Peach Pie

Southern peach pies are usually made with canned peaches in syrup, to ensure a wonderfully sweet pie year-round. This pie uses fresh. Southern peach pies are typically quite sweet. This one? Not so much. A Southern peach pie may also be heavily spiced with cinnamon, maybe even some nutmeg. This pie is delicately spiced with hardly more than a suggestion of cinnamon. Maybe I should rename this pie "Southern-Inspired Peach Pie." Either way, this pie takes advantage of those few short summer months when fuzzy peaches hang low off the trees, practically begging us to enjoy them in all their juicy glory. I will gladly oblige!

1 recipe Cornmeal Pie Dough (page 38)
  or Rich and Buttery Pie Dough (page 30)

½ cup sugar

¼ cup light brown sugar

3 tablespoons all-purpose flour

½ teaspoon ground cinnamon

Pinch of kosher salt

Approximately 2 pounds (7 or 8 medium) peaches, peeled, pitted, and cut into ¼-inch-thick slices (5 cups)

½ teaspoon almond extract

2 tablespoons unsalted butter, cut into ½-inch cubes

Optional
1 tablespoon heavy cream
1 tablespoon turbinado or sanding sugar

Preheat the oven to 425°F.

In a medium-size bowl, combine the sugars, flour, cinnamon, and salt, and mix well.

In a large mixing bowl, combine the sliced peaches, almond extract, and the sugar mixture. Toss gently, and set aside.

On a well-floured surface, roll out one portion of the dough until it is about ⅛-inch thick and will fit a 9-inch pie plate. Gently pick up the dough, center it over the pie plate, and ease it into the plate. Let the excess dough hang over the rim. Pour in the filling and spread it out evenly. Dot the surface of the filling with the butter.

Roll out the second portion of dough to the same size. Lay the dough over the filling, and trim the edges of both layers of dough to leave a 1-inch overhang. Pressing the edges together, fold them under, and then decoratively crimp the perimeter. With a sharp knife, cut 5 vents in the top crust.

Bake the pie for 15 minutes. Then reduce the heat to 375° and continue baking for 35 to 40 minutes, until the crust is golden brown. Let the pie cool to room temperature before enjoying.

Optional:
For a lovely sheen on the baked pie, use a pastry brush to paint the surface with the cream. If you like, sprinkle the sugar over the cream. As the pie bakes, the sugar will caramelize, and it will crackle when you slice a wedge of the freshly baked pie.

THICKENING FRUIT PIES

You have made a double-crusted pie. It is a thing of beauty. The crust is bumpy and burnished; the crimps have held their shape while in the oven. You set it on the kitchen counter and wait patiently for the pie to cool to room temperature before slicing and devouring it. You make the first cut, and there is no resistance. You make the second cut and the golden surface of the crust collapses, unleashing a tsunami of fruit juice. You lift the piece from the pie plate, only to find that the bottom crust is as damp as a wet tissue. Your filling has not thickened sufficiently. Your pie might still *taste* delicious, but let's just go ahead and say it: it has lost the power to impress your dinner guests. It has happened to the best of us.

There are a few ways to handle the problem of thickening. Some are useful, some not so much. Most of the fruit pies in this book are relatively runny. I enjoy eating a slightly messy, imperfect pie—there is beauty in the homemade aspect. If you decide that you want your pies to be denser or even gushier, by all means toy with the amounts of thickener. You will find exactly what you want.

PRECOOKING THE FILLING

When making a fruit pie, some bakers will tell you to cook all or a part of the filling prior to assembling and baking the pie. This thickens the juice, making a denser syrup. You won't see any precooked fillings in this book, though. To my mind, a fruit pie should be bright and as unadulterated as possible: just fruit, sugar, a bit of spice, and some added thickener.

MACERATING

Some bakers add a few extra tablespoons of sugar to particularly juicy slices of fruit, such as peaches or strawberries, and leave the fruit to sit for 15 to 30 minutes. The fruit releases a substantial amount of juice as it rests, which the baker then drains off and discards before baking. This has always seemed a bit counterintuitive to me. To throw away the essence of the fruit is to degrade your pie. However, there are exceptions to every rule: see the Sour Cherry Pie on page 149, where the potent elixir that results from concentrating the juices is used in a variety of ways and not just discarded.

ADDING STARCH

This is the method that I swear by. I rely on two starches: flour and cornstarch. Other bakers also use tapioca. Each has its strengths. There are times when I will use a combination of two starches.

FLOUR: Every pie baker has this on hand, which is a definite plus. The drawback to flour is that it will cloud an otherwise translucent filling, making it unwise to thicken a berry pie entirely with flour. Because of this, I frequently use a mixture of flour and cornstarch. Flour is the ideal thickener for apple pies, however, which contain rather opaque pieces of fruit.

CORNSTARCH: This thickener is flavorless, clear, and smooth, making it ideal for some berry pies. But be careful: cornstarch will not thicken highly acidic fruits, such as sour cherries or cranberries. Cornstarch also has twice the thickening power of flour, meaning you will need to use only half as much.

TAPIOCA: Tapioca, in flour or quick-cooking form, gives pies that shiny, almost commercial finish. But its thickening power diminishes over time, so the pie should be eaten relatively quickly. It is also important to let the fruit mingle with the tapioca for around 15 minutes before baking to soften the tapioca. Quick-cooking tapioca will leave little pearls of tapioca suspended in the thickened juice. I have always found this disconcerting, so that is why I have avoided it. You can, however, buy tapioca flour at an Asian grocery, or simply process quick-cooking tapioca in a coffee grinder or food processor, to solve this problem.

Green Tomato Pie

You might be familiar with fried green tomatoes—that oh-so-Southern dish of thickly sliced green tomatoes dredged in flour, then fried to a golden brown. Well, you can (and should!) serve green tomatoes beyond supper . . . how about nestled between two flaky layers of piecrust? This pie might sound peculiar, but it tastes very much like an apple pie, with the added delightfully chewy bite of tomato skin.

1 recipe Standard Pie Dough (page 28)

Approximately 2 pounds green tomatoes, cut in
  half and then cut into ¼-inch-thick slices (7 cups),
  and partially seeded (see Note)
¾ cup sugar
½ teaspoon ground cinnamon
3 tablespoons all-purpose flour
3 tablespoons cornstarch
Pinch of kosher salt

Optional
1 tablespoon heavy cream
1 tablespoon turbinado or sanding sugar

Preheat the oven to 425°F.

In a large mixing bowl, gently toss the tomatoes with the sugar, cinnamon, flour, cornstarch, and salt until they're well coated. Set aside.

On a well-floured surface, roll out one portion of the dough until it is about ⅛-inch thick and will fit a 9-inch pie plate. Gently pick up the dough, center it over the pie plate, and ease it into the plate. Let the excess dough hang over the rim. Pour in the filling and spread it out evenly.

Roll out the second portion of dough to the same size. Lay the dough over the filling, and trim the edges of both layers of dough to leave a 1-inch overhang. Pressing the edges together, fold them under, and then decoratively crimp the perimeter. With a sharp knife, cut 5 vents in the top crust.

Bake the pie for 15 minutes. Then reduce the heat to 375° and continue baking for 40 to 45 minutes, until the crust is golden brown. Let the pie cool to room temperature before enjoying.

Note: You'll notice that I have instructed you to **partially** *seed the tomatoes. That's because the pie can get too juicy if all the pulp and seeds are left in place. When you slice the tomatoes, leave on the cutting board whatever seeds and pulp fall from the fruit. This will ensure a perfectly juicy and flavorful pie.*

Optional:
For a lovely sheen on the baked pie, use a pastry brush to paint the surface with the cream. If you like, sprinkle the sugar over the cream. As the pie bakes, the sugar will caramelize, and it will crackle when you slice a wedge of the freshly baked pie.

Coconut Cream Pie

Like so many sweet and creamy pies the South has taken ownership of, this has been a standby for years, and with good reason. The combination of sweetened shredded coconut and rich cream gives this pie a chewiness that can't be beat! Never one to shy away from coconut, I updated this recipe by compounding the flavor, using coconut milk in addition to regular milk. Since this is a rich pie to begin with, I use "lite" coconut milk; it is still flavorful and rich, yet doesn't weigh down the pie.

1 Graham Cracker Crust (page 42) or Vanilla Wafer Crust (page 43)

For the filling
1½ cups "lite" coconut milk
1 cup whole milk
⅔ cup sugar
3 tablespoons cornstarch
3 large egg yolks, beaten
Pinch of kosher salt
1 tablespoon unsalted butter
1 teaspoon vanilla extract
¾ cup sweetened shredded coconut, toasted (see Note)

For the topping
½ cup heavy cream
2 teaspoons confectioners' sugar

Combine the coconut milk and whole milk in a medium-size saucepan and bring the mixture to a simmer over medium heat. Remove the milk mixture from the heat, and stir in the sugar until it's dissolved.

In a small bowl, combine ½ cup of the milk mixture with the cornstarch, and stir until smooth. In a separate small bowl, combine another ½ cup of the milk mixture with the egg yolks and salt to temper the yolks. Add both the cornstarch and the egg yolk mixtures to the saucepan, and stir into the remaining milk mixture.

Return the saucepan to medium heat, and cook the milk mixture, whisking constantly, until it comes to a boil. Reduce the heat to low and continue cooking until the mixture thickens, about 2 minutes. At this point, the mixture should have the consistency of a loose pudding that coats the back of a spoon. Remove the pan from the heat and stir in the butter and the vanilla. Reserve ¼ cup of the toasted coconut for garnish, and fold the remaining ½ cup into the pudding. Pour the pudding into the prepared pie shell. Place a piece of plastic wrap directly on the surface to prevent a skin from forming, and refrigerate until entirely chilled, about 4 hours.

When you are ready to serve the pie, combine the heavy cream and the confectioners' sugar in a bowl, and whip until it forms soft peaks. Remove the pie from the refrigerator and mound the whipped cream on top. Sprinkle the reserved coconut on top of the whipped cream, and serve.

Note:
To toast coconut, spread it out on a baking sheet and bake it in a preheated 325°F oven for 10 to 12 minutes, until golden brown.

Black Walnut Pie

Black walnuts are like "walnuts plus." They contain several times the amount of oil found in standard English walnuts and taste slightly vegetal. It's common to find black walnuts for sale pre-shelled and in pieces, due to the difficulty of processing the nuts. The shells have deep grooves, and the nuts cling steadfastly to them. The nut meat is bound in a bitter husk that must be removed, a process that leaves a sooty stain on the fingers—hence the name "black walnut."

Recipes for pies that feature black walnuts run the gamut from ones that are similar to pecan pie to pies flavored with molasses or even sorghum. But I wanted a unique pie recipe, one that celebrated the particularities of the walnut, and this is the one I came up with. A dense dessert, the filling contains dark chocolate chunks, which pair nicely with the strong flavor of the black walnuts. A smattering of raisins offers sweetness while cutting the richness of the nuts and the chocolate. Don't worry if you can't find black walnuts—the pie is also great made with English walnuts. Think of this pie as a hefty chocolate chunk cookie, and cut yourself a little slice. But beware: walnut-lovers adore this pie.

½ recipe Standard Pie Dough (page 28) or
Whole Wheat Pie Dough (page 40)

2 large eggs
½ cup sugar

¼ cup brown sugar

¼ teaspoon kosher salt

½ cup all-purpose flour

8 tablespoons (1 stick) unsalted butter, melted

1 teaspoon vanilla extract

1 cup roughly chopped black walnuts

1 cup semisweet or bittersweet chocolate chunks

⅓ cup raisins

Preheat the oven to 375°F.

On a well-floured surface, roll out the dough until it is about ⅛-inch thick and will fit a 9-inch pie plate. Gently pick up the dough, center it over the pie plate, and ease it into the plate. Trim the edges of the dough to leave a 1-inch overhang. Fold the edges under, and then decoratively crimp the perimeter. Return the pie shell to the refrigerator to chill until the filling is ready.

Combine the eggs, sugars, and salt in a large bowl, and using an electric mixer on high speed, beat until the mixture is light and fluffy, about 2 minutes. Add the flour, melted butter, and vanilla, and stir until smooth. Fold in the walnuts, chocolate chunks, and raisins.

Remove the pie shell from the refrigerator, and pour the filling into the shell, spreading it out evenly. Bake the pie for 40 to 45 minutes, until it's golden brown. Black walnut pie is equally delicious served warm or at room temperature.

Lemon Meringue Pie

Lemon meringue pie is a classic, but it has always seemed a shame to me that one of the main ingredients in the filling is water. I want my pie fillings to be rich, full of flavor, and creamy, not watery and gloppy. To that end, I substitute milk for the water. The milk imparts a lovely creaminess while the lemon maintains a tart punch. Some of you are probably wondering if the lemon juice will curdle the milk. I promise that it won't. When scalded and then mixed with the lemon juice, egg yolk, and cornstarch—the basis for the custard—the mixture does its magic and makes a sumptuous custard. I suppose that this pie is actually a reimagined classic. Some may want to rename it "Creamy Lemon Meringue Pie," but I just call it delicious.

½ recipe Standard Pie Dough (page 28) or Sour Cream
  Pie Dough (page 36)

For the filling
2 cups whole milk
⅔ cup sugar
4 large egg yolks
½ cup lemon juice (from approximately 4 lemons)
1 tablespoon grated lemon zest (from approximately
  2 lemons)
¼ cup cornstarch
Pinch of kosher salt
2 tablespoons unsalted butter
1 teaspoon vanilla extract

For the meringue
4 large egg whites, at room temperature
¼ teaspoon cream of tartar
Pinch of kosher salt
½ cup sugar
¾ teaspoon vanilla extract

Make the filling: Combine the milk and sugar in a medium-size saucepan. Bring the mixture to almost simmering over medium heat, stirring occasionally. Remove the saucepan from the heat and set aside.

In a medium-size bowl, combine the egg yolks, lemon juice, lemon zest, cornstarch, and salt, and whisk until smooth. To temper the yolks, add about ½ cup of the hot milk mixture to the yolk mixture, and whisk until smooth. Then slowly pour the yolk mixture into the remaining milk mixture. Stirring constantly, bring the mixture to a boil over medium heat, 3 to 4 minutes. The mixture should thicken substantially and coat the back of a spoon.

Pour the custard into a bowl, and stir in the butter and the vanilla. Place a piece of plastic wrap directly on the surface of the custard to prevent a skin from forming, and let it cool to room temperature. Then refrigerate the custard. (The filling can be prepared up to 1 day in advance.)

Prepare the pie shell: Preheat the oven to 400°F.

On a well-floured surface, roll out the dough until it is about ⅛-inch thick and will fit a 9-inch pie plate. Gently pick up the dough, center it over the pie plate, and ease it into the plate. Trim the edges of the dough to leave a 1-inch overhang. Fold the edges under, and then decoratively crimp the perimeter.

With the tines of a fork, prick the bottom of the pie shell in several places. Line the pie shell with a round of parchment paper cut to size. Pour in about 2 cups of dried beans (these can be reused), and bake the shell for 10 minutes. Remove the beans and parchment paper, and continue to bake the shell for another 8 to 10 minutes, until the crust is beginning to brown. Remove the pie crust from the oven and let it cool. Lower the oven heat to 350°.

Spoon the lemon custard into the cooled pie shell. Shake the pie plate gently to spread the filling evenly in the crust. Set aside.

Make the meringue: Using an electric mixer on high speed, beat the egg whites with the cream of tartar until frothy. Add the salt and continue beating. As the egg whites turn glossy, slowly add the sugar, 1 tablespoon at a time, incorporating each spoonful before adding the next. Continue to beat until the whites form stiff peaks but are not absolutely dry, about 4 minutes. Fold in the vanilla.

Spoon some of the meringue around the perimeter of the pie, and spread it until it touches the inner edge of the crust. (It is important to create a seal between the meringue and the crust, to protect against shrinkage.) Mound the rest of the meringue in the center, and then spread it out to meet the meringue along the perimeter. The meringue should cover the entire top of the pie.

Bake the pie for 10 to 15 minutes, until the meringue is golden brown. Remove the pie from the oven and let it cool to room temperature before enjoying.

MY MERINGUE IS WEEPING!

A *weeping meringue:* the phrase alone is fraught with emotion. Meringues can be delicate. They are sensitive to their environment. They can shrink. They can weep, which in turn can make the baker weep. But what exactly does it mean for a meringue to weep? Egg whites are a protein. When baked for too long, they contract, squeezing out their moisture. This moisture needs to go somewhere. Too often that "somewhere" means the top of the meringue, where the moisture gathers in beads, or the surface of the filling, where it pools in a syrupy slick. Here are some hints to help avoid this problem:

Make sure that your egg whites are at room temperature before you beat them. This helps the sugar melt, and helps prevent temperature shock upon baking.

Add a bit of a stabilizer, such as cream of tartar, to the egg whites as you beat them.

Add the sugar *slowly*, allowing it to dissolve. A good rule of thumb to test the sugar's dissolution is to gently rub a bit of the whipped egg whites between your fingers: there should be little to no grittiness. If there is some, simply beat the egg whites for a bit longer.

When placing the meringue on the pie, make sure to create a seal along the inner perimeter of the crust. No filling should be visible. This prevents shrinkage. Then mound the rest of the meringue in the center of the pie and work your way out to meet the edges.

Bake the meringue in a moderate (350°F) oven for 12 to 15 minutes to avoid overcooking.

Humidity plays a part. If it is humid outside, the pie will more than likely weep. You have two choices: either deal with it and enjoy the pie anyway, or make a non-meringue pie that day.

Meringue pies are delicious to eat, but their pleasures are admittedly fleeting. The short shelf life of a meringue pie makes it necessary to enjoy it as fast as you can. In fact, I suggest making the crust and filling for these kinds of pies in advance, while leaving the meringue topping off until a few hours before you're ready to serve. Then whip, mound, bake, and cool. That way you can avoid the weeping (from the pie and yourself) and everyone can enjoy the billowy masterpiece.

Blackberry Jam Pie

Imagine the best peanut butter and jelly sandwich that you have ever tasted: ethereal white bread, sweet jam with just the right number of seeds to stick in your teeth, and salty peanut butter. Now, take the peanut butter out of the equation, and that is what you get when you make this pie: a buoyant, jammy confection that is piled in a traditional salty short crust.

This pie was made by Mrs. H. V. Parsons and won the prize at the Louisiana State Fair. Her recipe has been passed down through her family for sixty-five years, and I can see why. It's both a luxurious and a simple pie. Because it calls for blackberry jam instead of fresh berries, you can make it even in the dead of winter, when the taste of fresh berries is a distant memory. The original recipe, in true Southern fashion, calls for a lot of sugar. I cut the sugar down. If you use a high-quality jam with minimal extra ingredients, the true berry flavor will shine through. The voluminous meringue adds a chewy crust, just like the bread in a jam sandwich.

½ recipe Standard Pie Dough (page 28)

For the filling
3 large egg yolks
¼ cup sugar
1 teaspoon vanilla extract
1 cup blackberry jam

2 tablespoons all-purpose flour
1 cup buttermilk

For the meringue
3 large egg whites, at room temperature
¼ teaspoon cream of tartar
Pinch of kosher salt
6 tablespoons sugar
½ teaspoon vanilla extract

Prepare the pie shell: Preheat the oven to 400°F. On a well-floured surface, roll out the dough until it is about ⅛-inch thick and will fit a 9-inch pie plate. Gently pick up the dough, center it over the pie plate, and ease it into the plate. Trim the edges of the dough to leave a 1-inch overhang. Fold the edges under, and then decoratively crimp the perimeter.

With the tines of a fork, prick the bottom of the pie shell in several places. Line the shell with a round of parchment paper cut to size. Pour in about 2 cups of dried beans (these can be reused), and bake the shell for 10 minutes. Remove the beans and parchment paper, and continue to bake the shell for another 8 to 10 minutes, until the crust is beginning to brown. Remove the piecrust from the oven and let it cool to room temperature while you make the filling.

Make the filling: Combine the egg yolks, sugar, vanilla, jam, flour, and buttermilk in the top of a double boiler, and mix well. Place the pan over simmering water and cook, whisking constantly, until the mixture thickens to a puddinglike consistency, about 7 minutes. Remove the pan from the heat, and continue to stir the custard until it cools slightly. Pour the custard into the cooled pie shell. Lay a sheet of plastic wrap directly over the surface of the filling to prevent a skin from forming, and let the pie cool to room temperature.

Make the meringue: Preheat the oven to 350°F.

Using an electric mixer on high speed, beat the egg whites with the cream of tartar until frothy. Add the salt and continue beating. As the egg whites turn glossy, slowly add the sugar, 1 tablespoon at a time, incorporating each spoonful before adding the next. Continue to beat until the whites form stiff peaks but are not absolutely dry, about 4 minutes. Fold in the vanilla.

Spoon some of the meringue around the perimeter of the pie, and spread it until it touches the inner edge of the crust. (It is important to create a seal between the meringue and the crust, to protect against shrinkage.) Mound the rest of the meringue in the center, and then spread it out to meet the meringue along the perimeter. The meringue should cover the entire top of the pie.

Bake the pie for 10 to 15 minutes, until the meringue is golden brown. Remove the pie from the oven and let it cool to room temperature before enjoying.

WHAT IS BLIND BAKING?

Blind baking refers to baking a piecrust before filling it. Though many pies that have a precooked filling (such as cream pies and meringue pies) call for a prebaked cookie or graham cracker crust, others call for a prebaked standard short crust. In order for an empty pie shell to maintain its shape as it bakes, the dough must be weighted. In kitchen supply stores you may see fancy boxes of terra-cotta spheres labeled as "pie weights." While you can definitely use these, pie weights don't have to be anything official. Dried beans or even rice, about 2 cups' worth, work just as well. They can even be cooled, stored, and reused for baking time and again.

Before you weigh down the crust, you need to put foil, or, better yet, parchment paper, into the shell in order to protect the dough from the pie weights. The reason I recommend parchment paper over foil is the condensation factor: when baking, the heat may attract beads of moisture to the foil. Parchment paper is dryer and more porous, and the result is a crisper crust. Crusts that are blind baked should be filled the same day.

Peanut Pie

On a stretch of Highway 460, smack-dab between Norfolk and Richmond, stands the Virginia Diner. Opened in 1929, and dishing out regional specialties such as cured Virginia ham served atop fluffy country biscuits, fried chicken dinners, and pulled pork sandwiches, this restaurant is also famous for its salty-sweet peanut pie, a crunchy dessert erupting with peanuts that satisfies even the sweetest tooth. While the recipe for the Virginia Diner's peanut pie is a closely guarded secret, I found numerous recipes for peanut pie in Southern cookbooks—after all, the South grows 99 percent of all the peanuts consumed in this country.

The chopped peanuts in this pie rise to the top of the filling as it bakes, creating an almost peanut-brittle-like shell. Some recipes I found suggested light corn syrup, others dark. But with its ability to keep this pie rich and deep, the murkier dark corn syrup won out for me. Every peanut-lover who has eaten this pie has declared this salty-sweet, chewy, candy-bar-like confection a success!

½ recipe Standard Pie Dough (page 28)

3 large eggs
½ cup dark brown sugar
1 cup dark corn syrup
4 tablespoons (½ stick) unsalted butter, melted
1 teaspoon kosher salt
1 teaspoon vanilla extract
1 cup coarsely chopped lightly salted peanuts

Preheat the oven to 375°F.

On a well-floured surface, roll out the dough until it is about ⅛-inch thick and will fit a 9-inch pie plate. Gently pick up the dough, center it over the pie plate, and ease it into the plate. Trim the edges of the dough to leave a 1-inch overhang. Fold the edges under, and then decoratively crimp the perimeter. Return the pie shell to the refrigerator to chill until the filling is ready.

In a large bowl, with an electric mixer set on high speed, beat the eggs until they're frothy, about 2 minutes. Add the brown sugar, corn syrup, melted butter, salt, and vanilla, and beat on medium speed for another 2 minutes or so, until thoroughly blended. Fold in the peanuts.

Remove the pie shell from the refrigerator, and pour the filling into the shell. Bake the pie for 45 to 50 minutes, until the top is lightly browned and the center is almost set. Remove the pie from the oven, and let it cool to room temperature before enjoying.

Pecan Pie

There are about as many pecan pie recipes out there as there are pecan pie lovers. In other words—a lot! While researching this book, I baked and ate my way through many of them (hey, it's a living!). Some I loved; some I felt simply moderate about. While chewing on the final bite of one of those slices of pie, I began to think about what separates the good from the great. Pecan pie is sweet—very sweet. The filling is almost confectionary, but the gooey sweetness plays so nicely with the nuts. I decided that the most successful pies were the nuttiest. How could I get the most impact from the nuts—that real toasted flavor? My answer was to toast the pecans before adding them to the pie. Toasting the nuts prior to baking releases their oils, deepening the flavor of the pie.

I also decided to chop the nuts. As lovely as a traditional pecan pie may look with pecans neatly tiling its surface, I have always found that consuming this dessert is a little unwieldy. Stabbing a nut with your fork is not the neatest activity, the filling oozes out the side, and the crust falls apart. Adding the chopped nuts to the buttery, sweet mixture allows for maximum nut impact. I do like to line the perimeter of the pie with untoasted pecan halves, however. They toast upon baking, and announce to diners the kind of sweet treat awaiting them.

½ recipe Standard Pie Dough (page 28) or Rich and Buttery Pie Dough (page 30)

1 cup (4 ounces) raw pecan halves, plus 15 to 20 extra
    halves

3 large eggs

2 tablespoons all-purpose flour

4 tablespoons (½ stick) unsalted butter, melted

⅔ cup brown sugar

¾ cup dark corn syrup

1 teaspoon vanilla extract

¼ teaspoon kosher salt

Preheat the oven to 350°F.

On a well-floured surface, roll out the dough until it is about ⅛-inch thick and will fit a 9-inch pie plate. Gently pick up the dough, center it over the pie plate, and ease it into the plate. Trim the edges of the dough to leave a 1-inch overhang. Fold the edges under, and then decoratively crimp the perimeter. Return the pie shell to the refrigerator to chill until the filling is ready.

Spread the 1 cup of pecan halves on a small baking sheet, and toast in the oven for 8 to 10 minutes, until browned and fragrant. Remove the pan, let the nuts cool slightly, and then coarsely chop them. Set aside.

Using an electric mixer or whisk, beat the eggs in a medium-size bowl. Add the flour, melted butter, brown sugar, corn syrup, vanilla, and salt, and stir until well combined. Fold in the chopped toasted pecans.

Remove the pie shell from the refrigerator and pour the filling into the shell. Gently arrange the reserved pecan halves in a single row around the perimeter of the pie, just inside the crust. Bake the pie for 45 to 50 minutes, until the crust is golden brown and the pecans are toasted. Remove the pie from the oven, and let it cool to room temperature before enjoying.

LET'S TALK ABOUT CORN SYRUP

Corn syrup: in recent years those two little words have earned themselves quite a reputation. In short, corn syrup is a sugarlike substance developed from cornstarch. Ounce for ounce it is about as sweet as sugar, but comes in a viscous syrup that prevents crystallization and keeps foods moist. Let's get something straight: corn syrup is not a *natural* substance, but it has been around, and baked with, in this country since the early twentieth century. There are two kinds of corn syrups available: light and dark. Light corn syrup is basically a clear liquid flavored with a bit of vanilla. It tastes like table sugar. Dark corn syrup is the color of maple syrup and has a rich, caramel-like taste. Do you love the smooth, sumptuous filling in pecan pie? Thank corn syrup. What about the smooth texture of a lollipop? It's the corn syrup that makes it a lollipop rather than crystallized rock candy. Many of the sweets we eat, and especially those with a smooth and tender mouthfeel, are made with corn syrup.

So what makes us utter those two words in hushed tones? While corn syrup itself may not be so terrible, its kin, high-fructose corn syrup, is the evil stepsister. To make high-fructose corn syrup, manufacturers process regular corn syrup, creating the enzymes fructose and glucose, the main ingredients in high-fructose corn syrup. While high-fructose corn syrup isn't sold directly to you, it is found in virtually every processed food that we consume. The U.S. Department of Agriculture subsidizes corn production but taxes imported sugar, making the use of high-fructose corn syrup cheaper for producers and less expensive to consumers. But the consumption of high-fructose corn syrup comes with its health risks—obesity, liver complications, and diabetes, to name a few.

A few recipes in this book use corn syrup. This book re-creates heirloom recipes. They are much-loved standards. So I opted to use the ingredients that were available to women in history, instead of finding substitutions. There really is no good substitute for the neutral, sweet flavor of corn syrup. However, if you find yourself desperate to maintain a diet of whole foods, honey or maple syrup simulates the texture of corn syrup (light and dark respectively), though they can't reproduce its flavor. This *is* a dessert cookbook, after all. No one ever got skinny off a piece of pie, but they did enjoy themselves while eating it. In this case, I repeat the golden rule immortalized by Julia Child and others: everything in moderation!

Chess Pie

Recipes for chess pie began appearing in community cookbooks in the late 1920s. The origin of the pie's name is something of a mystery, one that's hotly debated by food historians. Some think it's an elision of "cheese," a reference to the pie's soft curdlike texture that calls to mind a (cheese-less) cheesecake; others think it comes from "chest," because traditional versions of the pie contained so much sugar that they could be stored in a pie chest instead of the refrigerator.

But just what is a chess pie, anyway? Maybe the more appropriate question is what isn't a chess pie? Nothing—except the ingredients, usually pantry staples—is simple when it comes to chess pie. Where to begin? In its simplest terms, a chess pie is a sweet baked custard pie. But different recipes abound. Some include lemon juice or vinegar to cut the sweetness. Others include buttermilk, either a little or quite a lot—and then the pie is called Buttermilk Pie. I have seen a chocolate chess pie. There are chess pies chock-full of nuts. Some contain cream. Many of the custards are thickened with cornmeal. See what I mean? Coming up with a recipe can be a daunting task!

With all of this in mind, this is the recipe I have arrived at. It is sweet—sweeter than many other pies in this book, but less sweet than some chess pie recipes I came across. The pie is dairy-rich, sunny from eggs, and rich with butter and a bit of buttermilk. Thickened with both cornmeal and flour, the pie has grit and wobble. It is simple, sweet, and delightful—all the things that a Southern pie should be.

½ recipe Standard Pie Dough (page 28) or Sour Cream
  Pie Dough (page 36)

4 large eggs
1¼ cups sugar
4 tablespoons (½ stick) unsalted butter, melted
1 tablespoon cornmeal
1 tablespoon all-purpose flour
⅓ cup buttermilk
1½ teaspoons vanilla extract
½ teaspoon kosher salt

Preheat the oven to 350°F.

On a well-floured surface, roll out the dough until it is about ⅛-inch thick and will fit a 9-inch pie plate. Gently pick up the dough, center it over the pie plate, and ease it into the plate. Trim the edges of the dough to leave a 1-inch overhang. Fold the edges under, and then decoratively crimp the perimeter. Return the pie shell to the refrigerator to chill until the filling is ready.

In a medium-size bowl whisk the eggs until frothy. Beating well after each addition, add the sugar, melted butter, cornmeal, flour, buttermilk, vanilla, and salt. The filling should be fairly smooth when you're done.

Remove the pie shell from the refrigerator, and pour the filling into the shell. Bake the pie for approximately 40 minutes, until its center is almost set. The pie should still have a little jiggle to it—it will set more as it cools. Remove the pie from the oven, and let it cool to room temperature before enjoying.

Quince-Apple Pie

Quince trees used to flourish in the South. But because of a susceptibility to disease, they're rarer now than they used to be, and as a result, quince has fallen out of favor in the United States. But early in our country's history, settlers regularly baked, stewed, and poached quinces.

The quince is a strange fruit. You can't eat it out of hand—its skin is inedible and coated in a fine, dusty fur. It looks like a cross between an Anjou pear and a Golden Delicious apple, and it has an intoxicating, almost floral perfume. But uncooked, the flesh is so tart and astringent that if you took a bite you would probably spit it right out. When cooked, though, the fruit softens, changes flavor— becoming honeyed—and takes on a lovely rosy hue.

Because of these properties, the recipe for this pie is multipart, involving poaching, simmering, and, finally, baking. The quinces are sliced and poached in honey; the subtle, sweet flavor of the honey creates a wonderful parallel with the quince. And you will notice that this is not a pure quince pie. By mixing quince with fresh apple, the floral aspect of the fruit mellows a bit, and the apple lends the pie a tender bite.

1 recipe Whole Wheat Pie Dough (page 40) or
Rich and Buttery Pie Dough (page 30)

2 pounds quinces (4 or 5 medium quinces), peeled,
cored, and cut into ¼-inch-thick slices

½ cup honey

2 teaspoons vanilla extract

Pinch of kosher salt

Approximately 2 medium baking apples, such as
    Granny Smith, peeled, cored, and cut into
    ¼-inch-thick slices (2 cups)

½ cup sugar

Grated zest and juice of 1 medium lemon

2 tablespoons all-purpose flour

2 tablespoons unsalted butter, cut into ½-inch cubes

Optional

1 tablespoon heavy cream

1 tablespoon turbinado or sanding sugar

In a large saucepan or Dutch oven, combine the quince slices with 1½ cups of water and the honey, vanilla, and salt. Bring the mixture to a boil over high heat. Then reduce the heat to a simmer, cover the pan, and cook, stirring occasionally, for approximately 20 minutes. The quince slices should be fork-tender but still retain their shape. Drain, reserving the cooking liquid, and set the quince aside to cool. Return the liquid to a saucepan, bring it to a vigorous boil over high heat, and boil until the liquid has reduced by half, 5 to 7 minutes.

Meanwhile, preheat the oven to 425°F.

In a large bowl, combine the quince, apples, sugar, lemon juice and zest, and flour with ¼ cup of the poaching liquid and toss gently. Set aside.

On a well-floured surface, roll out one portion of the dough until it is about ⅛-inch thick and will fit a 9-inch pie plate.

Optional:

For a lovely sheen on the baked pie, use a pastry brush to paint the surface with the cream. If you like, sprinkle the sugar over the cream. As the pie bakes, the sugar will caramelize, and it will crackle when you slice a wedge of the freshly baked pie.

Gently pick up the dough, center it over the pie plate, and ease it into the plate. Let the excess dough hang over the rim. Pour in the filling and spread it out evenly. Dot the surface of the filling with the butter.

Roll out the second portion of dough to the same size. Lay the dough over the filling, and trim the edges of both layers of dough to leave a 1-inch overhang. Pressing the edges together, fold them under, and then decoratively crimp the perimeter. With a sharp knife, cut 5 vents in the top crust.

Bake the pie for 15 minutes. Then reduce the heat to 375° and continue baking for 40 to 45 minutes, until the crust is golden brown. Let the pie cool to room temperature before enjoying.

Sweet Potato Meringue Pie

Much like sweet tea, fried chicken, and hush puppies, sweet potato pie is a culinary tradition in the South. Think of the sweet potato pie—with its ruddy color, substantial starchy filling, and seasoning of warm spices—as the South's answer to the North's pumpkin pie. A careless diner might even confuse the two. But the sweet potato pie, a crowning finale to any Southern feast, is definitely a dessert that stands on its own—especially when topped with marshmallow-like meringue. Of course the meringue in this recipe serves no purpose other than culinary embellishment. Looking through the sweet potato pie recipes in my cookbooks, I saw that there was an even split between the meringue-lovers and the naysayers. I guess you can count me as one of the lovers. The meringue is buoyant and the filling is silky—sounds like a pretty good match to me.

½ recipe Standard Pie Dough (page 28) or
    Leaf Lard Pie Dough (page 32)

For the filling
2 cups mashed sweet potato (see Note)
¾ cup whole milk
3 large eggs, beaten
½ cup sugar
½ cup brown sugar
½ teaspoon ground cinnamon
1 teaspoon ground ginger
Pinch of kosher salt

For the meringue
3 large egg whites, at room temperature
¼ teaspoon cream of tartar
Pinch of kosher salt
6 tablespoons sugar
½ teaspoon vanilla extract

Preheat the oven to 350°F.

On a well-floured surface, roll out the dough until it is about ⅛-inch thick and will fit a 9-inch pie plate. Gently pick up the dough, center it over the pie plate, and ease it into the plate. Trim the edges of the dough to leave a 1-inch overhang. Fold the edges under, and then decoratively crimp the perimeter. Return the pie shell to the refrigerator to chill until the filling is ready.

Make the filling: Combine the mashed sweet potatoes, milk, and eggs in a medium-size bowl and stir well. Add the sugars, cinnamon, ginger, and salt, and stir well to combine.

Remove the pie shell from the refrigerator, and pour the filling into the shell. Bake the pie for 45 to 50 minutes. The filling should still be slightly wobbly in the center. Remove the pie from the oven, and let it cool while you make the meringue. Leave the oven set to 350°.

Make the meringue: Using an electric mixer on high speed, beat the egg whites with the cream of tartar until frothy. Add the salt and continue beating. As the egg whites turn glossy, slowly add the sugar, 1 tablespoon at a time, incorporating each spoonful before adding the next. Continue to beat until the whites form stiff peaks but are not absolutely dry, about 4 minutes. Fold in the vanilla.

Note:
To bake and mash a sweet potato, preheat the oven to 375°F. Prick the sweet potato a few times with a fork, then bake as you would a regular potato, for approximately 1 hour. Let it cool slightly, and then squeeze the flesh from the sweet potato, discarding the skin. With a hand masher or a fork, mash the potato until almost smooth. About 4 medium sweet potatoes yield 2 cups mashed.

134

Spoon some of the meringue around the perimeter of the pie. Spread it until it touches the inner edge of the crust. (It is important to create a seal between the meringue and the crust, to protect against shrinkage.) Mound the rest of the meringue in the center, and then spread it out to meet the meringue along the perimeter. The meringue should cover the entire top of the pie.

Bake the pie for 10 to 15 minutes, until the meringue is golden brown. Remove the pie from the oven and let it cool to room temperature before enjoying.

Tar Heel Pie

North Carolina has been known as the Tar Heel State since the Civil War, thanks to the numerous pine tree forests that produce large quantities of tar, rosin, turpentine, and pitch. This pie may not be an heirloom pie, but it has become a favorite of North Carolinians over the past few decades. The brownie filling is reminiscent of thick, dark tar. Easy to make, with melted chocolate and butter stirred in one bowl, this sinfully rich pie looks impressive and tastes decadent. Traditional recipes for Tar Heel pie don't call for the addition of coffee—that's my innovation. The coffee granules don't really make the pie mocha-flavored, but rather deepen the chocolate flavor.

½ recipe Standard Pie Dough (page 28)

8 tablespoons (1 stick) unsalted butter, melted
1 cup semisweet chocolate chips, or 6 ounces
    semisweet chocolate, chopped
⅓ cup all-purpose flour
½ cup sugar
½ cup light brown sugar
2 large eggs
1 cup roughly chopped pecans
1 teaspoon vanilla extract
1 teaspoon instant coffee granules
Pinch of kosher salt

136

Preheat the oven to 350°F.

On a well-floured surface, roll out the dough until it is about ⅛-inch thick and will fit a 9-inch pie plate. Gently pick up the dough, center it over the pie plate, and ease it into the plate. Trim the edges of the dough to leave a 1-inch overhang. Fold the edges under, and then decoratively crimp the perimeter. Return the pie shell to the refrigerator to chill until the filling is ready.

In a medium-size bowl, pour the warm melted butter over the chocolate chips. Stir occasionally until the chocolate is melted and the butter and chocolate are well combined. Add each of the remaining ingredients to the chocolate-butter mixture, stirring well after each addition.

Remove the pie shell from the refrigerator, and pour the filling into the shell. Shake the pie plate gently to spread the filling evenly. Bake the pie for 35 to 40 minutes, until the crust is golden brown and the filling is set. Remove the pie from the oven and let it cool for at least 1 hour before serving.

Banana Cream Pie

Though bananas are not native to the United States—the fruit was first imported to the States in the mid-nineteenth century—banana cream pie is now a classic of Southern cuisine. Southerners love their sweet pies, and banana cream pie is no exception. Usually the filling is simply vanilla pudding layered with sliced bananas and topped with mounds of whipped cream. While this combination is delicious in its own right, there are times when it gets excessive. My take on this classic, though hardly austere, is more about balanced composition than sweetness. This dessert is not so much a pie as it is a layering of tastes and textures.

The crust is a crumbly shell of vanilla wafers with just a hint of salt, which is then topped with a thin layer of semisweet chocolate ganache. The chocolate is rich and dark, a somber note in the pie. Next comes the star of the show—the bananas—sandwiched under a cumulus cloud of vanilla pudding. After this has been thoroughly chilled comes the layer of whipped cream. It is important that the cream be whipped *sans* sweetener; it offers a neutral ballast to the pie's airy sweetness. You can shave a bit of chocolate over this pie before serving it, as a suggestion of what it contains. Some might say that this is gilding the lily, but I say, gild away!

1 Vanilla Wafer Crust (page 43)

For the ganache
2 ounces semisweet chocolate, chopped
⅓ cup heavy cream

For the filling
2 cups whole milk
2 large egg yolks
½ cup sugar
2 tablespoons all-purpose flour
1 tablespoon cornstarch
Pinch of kosher salt
2 tablespoons unsalted butter
1½ teaspoons vanilla extract
2 medium ripe bananas, peeled and sliced into ¼-inch-
    thick disks

For the top layer
½ cup heavy cream

Make the ganache: Place the chopped chocolate in a medium-size heatproof bowl. In a small saucepan, bring the cream to a boil. Pour the cream over the chocolate and let it sit for a moment, to begin melting the chocolate. With a rubber spatula, stir the chocolate slowly to further melt it and to incorporate the cream.

Spoon the ganache over the bottom of the prepared crust, spreading it out in an even layer with the spatula. Refrigerate the ganache-lined shell while you make the filling.

Make the filling: In a small saucepan, heat the milk until almost boiling. Remove the pan from the heat and set it aside. In a medium mixing bowl, combine the egg yolks, sugar, flour, cornstarch, and salt, and stir well. Slowly pour the scalded milk into the egg mixture, stirring constantly. Pour the mixture into the top of a double boiler and place it over simmering water. Cook, whisking constantly, until the mixture thickens to a custardlike consistency, about 7 minutes. Take the custard off the heat, and stir in the butter and the vanilla until the butter melts. Allow the custard to cool slightly on the counter, about 30 minutes.

Assemble the pie: Remove the ganache-lined crust from the refrigerator. Arrange the banana slices in a single layer over the ganache. Carefully pour in the custard; it should completely cover the bananas and fill the crust. Return the pie to the refrigerator to chill for a minimum of 4 hours or as long as 1 day.

When you are ready to serve the pie, remove it from the refrigerator. Whip the cream until it forms soft peaks. Mound the whipped cream on top of the custard, and serve.

Note:
To make chocolate curls to top the whipped cream, use a vegetable peeler to shave a bar of dark chocolate.

PIES
of the
MIDWEST

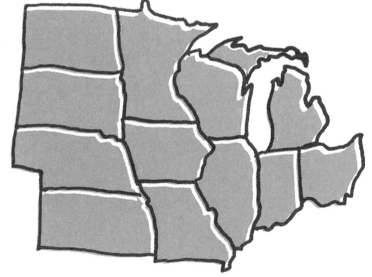

Indulgent cream pies and ingenious

meringues are hallmarks of the Midwest's pie-making tradition. Long winters meant a shortage of fresh fruit, and up until the mid-twentieth century, the Great Lakes region boasted the highest per capita acreage of pastureland and dairy farms in the United States. With plentiful milk and cream available, rural farmwives created rich, delicious desserts as the culmination to hearty dinners (it takes a lot of calories to farm).

But when the season allows, Midwestern pies celebrate produce, from tart rhubarb to Indiana's native persimmons to sour cherries plucked from the orchards that line the banks of Lake Michigan. In fact, almost all the cherry pie that we consume in this country is made with sour cherries. This tart cousin of the Bing cherry (the most common eat-out-of-hand variety) is sour in a mouth-pursing, puckery sort of way and not at all acrid. Many people eat sour cherries straight from the tree for a jolt of cherry flavor. Sour cherries are smaller than Bings and they don't cling to their pits as steadfastly. When mixed with sugar and baked in a pie, the sour cherry loses its sour factor and takes on a commanding cherriness, bright and juicy, that screams of summer.

If the Lower Peninsula of the state of Michigan looks like a left-hand mitten, then Traverse City, the sour cherry capital of America, lies between its ring and pinkie fingers. With a burgeoning local food movement and wineries dappling its sloping hills, the greater Traverse City area is sort of the Napa Valley of the Midwest. But Michiganders know that it's not wine that draws people to this region year after year. It's the sour cherry. There is much to be done with this little stalwart of summer. It is dried, made into jam, baked in cookies—and, of course, there is pie.

Baking pie with such an acidic fruit poses some problems. There is a thickener conundrum. The usual thickeners just won't do. Because of the high acid content of sour cherries, cornstarch accomplishes almost nothing. Too much flour will cloud the dazzling juice. Then there is tapioca. This thickener will always do the trick. The pie's juice will be rosy and clear, but if you're anything like me, you can never fully adjust to those little pearls gazing back at you like a million tiny eyeballs. One by one, I tried each thickener, but none of them was just right. Luckily, Andy Case at the Cherry Hut restaurant was more than happy to offer me a few pointers.

Just forty minutes southeast of the relative hustle and bustle of Traverse City, the Cherry Hut is a true piece of Americana. Nestled in the tiny village of Beulah (population 395), the restaurant started life as a seasonal pie shack. When the Kraker family opened the Cherry Hut in 1922, it sold only one thing: cherry pie. In 1935 the pie shack moved to its current location and launched an expanded menu to match its expanded facilities: besides pie, you could order a turkey sandwich and drip coffee.

In 1959, after managing the restaurant for two years, Leonard Case Jr. bought the establishment from the Krakers, and it's been in the Case family ever since. Leonard was a local Beulah boy who had worked in some capacity at the Cherry Hut since 1946. These days, Leonard's son, Andy, manages the restaurant, and the Cherry Hut is a one-stop cherry emporium: they make their own cherry jelly, jam, and preserves, and, of course, their famous sour cherry pie.

It's early in the season when I arrive at the Cherry Hut. The sky is vast and heavy. There's still a nip in the air, indicating the passing of a long and brutal winter. The rickety farm stands along Route 31 are selling mounds of strawberries and piles of local asparagus that look like helter-skelter stacks of pick-up-sticks. I know I've reached my destination as soon as I see the Cherry Hut's elevated sign—there's *no way* I could miss it. A huge image of Cherry Jerry the Pie-Faced Boy, the restaurant's mascot (imagine a jack-o'-lantern face with scalloped edges, painted cherry red, and you have the right idea), greets you as you exit the highway. The interior of the Cherry Hut is decked out in cherry paraphernalia: wallpaper featuring bunches of cherries hangs above red leatherette banquettes, the rose-colored carpet resembles cherry-stained clothes, and Cherry Jerry smiles back at diners from the placemats-cum-menus.

As I sit at a table with Andy, he graciously slides a glass of crimson house-made cherry ade—a beverage made from the macerating liquid of sour cherries—in front of me. Andy tells me a little bit about the history of the restaurant, and specifically the pie, as a waiter brings me a warm slice. "It's a good pie," he says modestly, "but I think we're selling more of a memory . . . nostalgia." I can see what he means. So much about the foods we love is tied to our recollections of eating them year after year. And in a vacation spot like Beulah, a place where grandparents bring their grandchildren each summer to swim in Crystal Lake, a slice of cherry pie from the Cherry Hut *is* about creating those memories.

The recipe for this pie hasn't changed much since Dorothy Kraker first began making it in 1922. It's a comparatively small pie at 8 inches in diameter, but each pie is cut into just four healthy pieces for serving. The crust is a lard crust, which makes it flaky and tender, and the filling—well, it's just cherries. This pie could be an advertisement for the Michigan Sour Cherry Board. When you sit down in front of a slice of the Cherry Hut's pie, you must put all other cherry pies, with their gloppy shellacked fillings, out of your mind. I do just that as I bring my fork down on my slice. Cherries tumble out and pool on the plate. The pie just holds together. And its flavor is pure, sweet, overflowing with fruitiness with just the right amount of tang. This is the sort of sour cherry pie that I'm dying to make. Although the pie comes from a well-established family restaurant, it has the homemade appeal of tradition.

Andy and I get to talking cherries. Or rather, I begin complaining about my difficulty making the perfect filling and Andy calmly gives me an education. Andy is a measured man, businesslike and composed; an education from him is a confidence-building exercise. As I regale him with stories of my filling nightmares, finally arriving at the unsatisfying and thus temporary tapioca solution, he nods solemnly. And then he begins to school me in the art of making a Cherry Hut pie.

At the Hut they use the Montmorency variety of sour cherries. This cherry is, of course, local and processed minimally. The fruit arrives mechanically pitted (the most taxing and staining part of the entire pie-making process) at the Cherry Hut. The pitted cherries are mixed with sugar and then flash-frozen. Sour cherry season is brief—the Hut has just two weeks to obtain all of their cherries for a year. From May through October, the kitchen averages about three hundred cherry pies a day. Each pie contains about one pound of pitted cherries.

Before the Cherry Hut bakers make a pie, they thaw the frozen cherry-sugar mixture and—here's the clincher—drain it. When I first hear this, it strikes me as deeply counter-intuitive, wasteful even. But Andy explains that the Cherry Hut uses the sweet ruby nectar to make jelly and the delicious cherry ade I've been gulping down. Nothing is wasted. Macerating the fruit softens it—the key to the Cherry Hut's pie. I learn that before baking, I don't want the fruit too firm. Firmness equals juiciness. In my own cherry-pie-making travails, my aim was to keep the fruit intact, when what I really needed was relaxed, almost sleepy fruit. Andy reassured me that if I tried this method, my pie would still be bursting with flavor, the cherries still plump. Sour cherries are such an assertive fruit that the pie I made would still taste strongly of cherries. One bite of a Cherry Hut pie assured me that this was the case. Sitting there at the restaurant, with Andy's tutelage under my belt and an almost clean plate in front of me, I knew what I had to do: go home and bake my own sour cherry pie, Cherry Hut style.

Sour Cherry Pie

This pie takes a while, but it is well worth the wait. The liquid that is left behind from macerating the cherries is superb—soft pink, overflowing with cherry flavor—and should definitely not be discarded. Mixed with seltzer it makes a refreshing quencher, or for something a little naughtier, try it mixed with vodka or brandy as a summer cocktail.

1 recipe Standard Pie Dough (page 28) or
   Leaf Lard Pie Dough (page 32)

4 cups pitted sour cherries (from about
   2 pounds fruit)
1¼ cups sugar
2 tablespoons all-purpose flour
¼ teaspoon almond extract
Pinch of kosher salt
2 tablespoons unsalted butter, cut into
   ½-inch cubes

Optional
1 tablespoon heavy cream
1 tablespoon turbinado or sanding sugar

Macerate the cherries: In a large bowl, mix the pitted cherries and ¾ cup of the sugar. Let the cherries macerate for at least 8 hours, or as long as overnight.

Pour the cherries and their juices into a large strainer set over a bowl and drain well, reserving the liquid to make cherry ade. Set the drained cherries aside.

Make the pie: Preheat the oven to 425°F.

In a large bowl, combine the cherries, the remaining ½ cup of sugar, and the flour, almond extract, and salt. Toss gently to mix.

On a well-floured surface, roll out one portion of the dough until it is about ⅛-inch thick and will fit a 9-inch pie plate. Gently pick up the dough, center it over the pie plate, and ease it into the plate. Let the excess dough hang over the rim. Pour in the filling and shake the pie plate gently to distribute it evenly. Dot the surface of the filling with the butter.

Roll out the second portion of dough to the same size. Lay the dough over the filling, and trim the edges of both layers of dough to leave a 1-inch overhang. Pressing the edges together, fold them under, and then decoratively crimp the perimeter. With a sharp knife, cut 5 vents in the top crust.

Bake the pie for 15 minutes. Then reduce the heat to 375° and continue baking for another 45 to 50 minutes, until the crust is golden brown. Let the pie cool to room temperature before enjoying.

Optional:
For a lovely sheen on the baked pie, use a pastry brush to paint the surface with the cream. If you like, sprinkle the sugar over the cream. As the pie bakes, the sugar will caramelize, and it will crackle when you slice a wedge of the freshly baked pie.

Ohio Shaker Lemon Pie

In the Shaker communities of the eighteenth and nineteenth centuries, working well was an act of prayer. There was beauty in their creations, like the clean lines of their slat-backed chairs and their oval storage boxes. These values carried into their baking as well, with a pie that wholeheartedly embraces the Shaker values of frugality and simplicity.

This pie has only two lemons in it, but it makes use of the entire fruit, peel and all, by macerating it in sugar. The rest of the pie is relatively simple: a few eggs, some flour, and since I'm not a Shaker, a bit of butter added for richness. While Shaker communities were dispersed throughout the Midwest, this recipe is distinctly Ohioan with the additional ingredient of flour, making it a more supple dessert. What you get is a delicious pie with a distinct lemon flavor and a pleasing snap from the pith in the fruit.

This pie requires a bit of advance preparation because the lemons need to macerate for a minimum of eight hours.

1 recipe Standard Pie Dough (page 28)

2 lemons, washed thoroughly
1¾ cups sugar
½ teaspoon kosher salt
4 large eggs
3 tablespoons unsalted butter, melted
3 tablespoons all-purpose flour

151

1 tablespoon heavy cream

1 tablespoon turbinado or sanding sugar

Bring a large saucepan of water to a boil. Blanch the lemons by submerging them in the boiling water for 30 seconds. Then remove the lemons and rinse them under cold water until they are cool to the touch. Trim and discard the ends of each lemon, and then cut each lemon in half lengthwise. With a sharp knife, cut the lemon halves crosswise into paper-thin slices, the thinner the better. (It is important to slice the lemons as thin as possible; otherwise, they may not break down adequately during the macerating process.) Discard any seeds.

Place the lemon slices in a nonreactive bowl. Add the sugar and the salt, and mix well. Cover the bowl with plastic wrap and let it rest at room temperature for 1 hour. Then stir the lemons once, cover the bowl again, and let it sit at room temperature overnight, or for a minimum of 8 hours.

When the lemons are ready, preheat the oven to 425°F.

In a medium-size bowl, lightly beat the eggs. Add the melted butter and the flour, stirring to combine. Pour the egg mixture over the lemons, mixing well to evenly disperse the lemon slices. Set aside.

On a well-floured surface, roll out one portion of the dough until it is about ⅛-inch thick and will fit a 9-inch pie plate. Gently pick up the dough, center it over the pie plate, and ease it into the plate. Let the excess dough hang over the rim. Pour in the filling and spread it out evenly.

Roll out the second portion of dough to the same size. Lay

Optional:

For a lovely sheen on the baked pie, use a pastry brush to paint the surface with the cream. If you like, sprinkle the sugar over the cream. As the pie bakes, the sugar will caramelize, and it will crackle when you slice a wedge of the freshly baked pie.

the dough over the filling. Trim the edges of both layers of dough to leave a 1-inch overhang. Pressing the edges together, fold them under, and then decoratively crimp the perimeter. With a sharp knife, cut 5 vents in the top crust.

Bake the pie for 25 minutes. Then reduce the heat to 350° and continue baking for another 25 minutes or until the top crust is golden brown. (If the crust begins to brown too quickly, tent it with a piece of aluminum foil for the duration of the baking time.) Let the pie cool to room temperature before enjoying.

Creamy Eggnog Pie

This festive pie takes advantage of the eggnog that lines the dairy aisle of every supermarket from Thanksgiving to New Year's. I like to pair the eggnog filling with a gingersnap crust; the spiciness of the eggnog plays nicely off the ginger in the crushed cookies. Garnish the whole thing with a dusting of freshly grated nutmeg, and it is time to ring in the holidays!

1 Gingersnap Crust (page 44)

1 envelope (¼ ounce) unflavored gelatin
3 tablespoons whole milk
2 cups store-bought eggnog
¼ cup sugar
2 teaspoons vanilla extract
1 tablespoon brandy
Pinch of kosher salt
½ cup heavy cream
Freshly grated nutmeg (see page 155), for garnish

In a small bowl, dissolve the gelatin in the milk. The mixture will thicken substantially.

Pour the eggnog into a medium-size saucepan and set it over low heat. Add the gelatin mixture, and stirring constantly, bring the eggnog almost to a boil, ensuring the gelatin is completely dissolved. Remove from the heat.

Pour the eggnog mixture into a bowl and chill it in the refrigerator, stirring it occasionally, for about 45 minutes, until it is just barely set. This step is important. You are not making eggnog-flavored Jell-O; you do not want the mixture to set entirely. Keep an eye on it, and when it is still viscous and resembles unbeaten egg whites, remove it from the refrigerator.

Using an electric mixer on medium speed, beat the eggnog mixture until it's smooth but still thick. Add the sugar, vanilla, brandy, and salt, and beat again until combined. Set aside.

In a medium-size bowl, whip the cream until it forms stiff peaks. The cream should be slightly more whipped than if you were to use it as a topping. Fold the whipped cream into the eggnog mixture until well combined.

Pour the eggnog-cream mixture into the gingersnap crust, spreading it out evenly with an offset spatula. Return the pie to the refrigerator to cool completely, about 3 hours.

Before serving, grate a dusting of nutmeg over the surface of the pie.

NUTMEG

Nutmeg is both more flavorful and more economical when purchased whole and ground for each use. A fragrant, warm, and slightly sweet spice, it quickly loses its potency once it is ground, and a jar of preground nutmeg is likely to turn to sawdust long before you'll make use of the whole thing. The whole nutmeg can be ground by rubbing the nut on a special nutmeg grinder or, easier still, on a Microplane grater.

Poppy Seed Pie

Poppy seed pie has been a mainstay on the menu at Rudy's Diner, a family-run institution in Brillion, Wisconsin, for more than sixty years. I discovered the recipe for this unexpected pie in Joanne Raetz Stuttgen and Terese Allen's Cafe Wisconsin Cookbook, *a compendium of Badger State diner and roadhouse specialties.*

My first association with poppy seed–centric desserts is with Eastern European–style Danishes and their dense, sweet, and sticky filling. This pie bears no resemblance to those old-school pastries. Essentially, this is a cream pie: poppy seeds are folded into a simple vanilla pudding and the cooled pie is crowned with whipped cream and garnished with more seeds. There's only a tablespoon of poppy seeds mixed into the pudding, and half that much used as a garnish. The seeds are crunchy, popping under your tongue, but in terms of flavor, the poppy seeds play more of a supporting role, letting the custard take center stage. The pie is delicately sweet, almost refreshing.

1 Graham Cracker Crust (page 42) or
   Vanilla Wafer Crust (page 43)

3 large egg yolks
3 tablespoons cornstarch
2 cups whole milk
½ cup sugar
Pinch of kosher salt
1 teaspoon vanilla extract
1½ tablespoons poppy seeds

1 cup heavy cream
3 tablespoons confectioners' sugar

Combine the egg yolks, cornstarch, and ¼ cup of water in a small bowl, and beat until smooth.

In a medium-size saucepan, combine the milk, sugar, salt, and vanilla, and bring to a simmer over medium-low heat, stirring often. Remove from the heat.

Slowly add approximately ½ cup of the hot milk mixture to the egg yolk mixture, whisking constantly until smooth. Slowly pour the egg yolk mixture into the remaining milk mixture in the saucepan. Return the pan to medium heat and bring the mixture to a boil, stirring constantly. The mixture will thicken substantially and should coat the back of a spoon.

Remove the pan from the heat, and stir 1 tablespoon of the poppy seeds into the custard. Then pour the custard into the prepared crust. Place a piece of plastic wrap directly on the surface of the custard to prevent a skin from forming, and allow it to cool to room temperature. Once the pie has reached room temperature, place it in the refrigerator. The pie will keep for a day up to this point.

When you're ready to serve the pie, remove it from the refrigerator. In a medium-size bowl, combine the cream and the confectioners' sugar. Whip the cream until it forms soft peaks. Mound the whipped cream on top of the custard, sprinkle with the remaining ½ tablespoon of poppy seeds, and serve.

TEMPERING

When making creams and custards, the technique of slowly stirring some of the hot milk mixture into the raw eggs or egg yolks is called tempering. *This raises the temperature of the eggs, ensuring a smooth emulsion when the eggs are stirred into the hot milk. If you add cold eggs to hot milk, you risk having a curdled or scrambled mixture.*

Hoosier Cream Pie

This pie is a truly regional specialty. It is so regional that most people outside of Indiana have never even heard of it. But mention this heirloom pie to a person from Indiana and I bet they can tell you all about it. In fact, this simple cream pie is so popular there that in 2009 the state named it the official state pie. Also called "desperation pie," this dessert is made with just three basic ingredients—cream, sugar, and flour—hence the "desperation." A true Hoosier cream pie contains no eggs, just heavy cream and flour. These two ingredients act almost like a roux, thickening and eventually baking into a dense custardlike filling.

If you choose to make this pie, know that there is no low-fat version. Milk or even half-and-half cannot be substituted for the heavy cream. Because the pie contains no eggs, the milk solids in the cream are crucial to the pie's setting. Remove the pie from the oven when the center still jiggles a bit—it will continue to set as it cools.

½ recipe Standard Pie Dough (page 28)

½ cup sugar
¼ cup light brown sugar
⅓ cup all-purpose flour
Pinch of kosher salt
2 cups heavy cream
½ teaspoon vanilla extract

Sprinkling of ground nutmeg, preferably freshly
grated (see page 155)

Preheat the oven to 425°F.

On a well-floured surface, roll out the dough until it is about
⅛-inch thick and will fit a 9-inch pie plate. Gently pick up the
dough, center it over the pie plate, and ease it into the plate.
Trim the edges of the dough to leave a 1-inch overhang. Fold
the edges under, and then decoratively crimp the perimeter.
Return the pie shell to the refrigerator to chill until the filling
is ready.

In a medium-size bowl, combine the sugars, flour, and salt,
and stir to mix. Add the cream and vanilla, and stir to mix
well. Let the mixture rest for about 5 minutes, allowing the
sugar to begin to melt.

Remove the pie shell from the refrigerator. Stir the filling
again to ensure that the ingredients are well blended, and then
pour the filling into the shell. Sprinkle nutmeg over the surface. Bake the pie for 10 minutes. Then reduce the heat to 350°
and continue baking for another 25 to 30 minutes, until the
filling is lightly browned. Jiggle the pie plate gently to test for
doneness: the filling should still move slightly but should not be
entirely liquid. Remove the pie from the oven, and let it cool to
room temperature before enjoying.

Burnt Sugar Meringue Pie

In Kansas they know a thing or two about making creamy desserts, and burnt sugar meringue pie is one of the best. Made with pantry staples and treated with care, this recipe transforms ordinary sugar into a deep caramel-infused custard. The meringue adds an ethereal touch—and is also a smart way of using up the whites left after separating the eggs for the custard.

I discovered this recipe in The Kansas Cookbook *by Frank Carey and Jayni Naas. The pie is credited to Twila Roenne of Osborne, Kansas. Like so many families from the Midwest, the Roenne family emigrated from Eastern Europe in the mid-nineteenth century. According to Twila, her father first tasted this pie in 1928, when he was working on a threshing crew at a neighbor's farm and the farmer's wife served it to them on their lunch break. Twila's father liked the pie so much, he brought the recipe home to her mother, who in turn taught it to Twila.*

The original recipe calls for a traditional short crust, but I think that the crumbly texture of a graham cracker crust is a more pleasant foil for this dense pie. I also tempered the pie's sweetness while heightening its wonderful flavor of burnt sugar.

1 Graham Cracker Crust (page 42)

For the filling
2½ cups whole milk
⅔ cup plus ½ cup sugar

⅓ cup all-purpose flour

½ teaspoon kosher salt

3 large egg yolks, beaten

1 teaspoon vanilla extract

For the meringue

3 large egg whites, at room temperature

¼ teaspoon cream of tartar

Pinch of kosher salt

6 tablespoons sugar

½ teaspoon vanilla extract

Make the filling: In a medium-size saucepan, bring the milk just to a simmer over low heat. When the milk reaches a simmer, remove it from the heat.

In another medium-size saucepan, warm the ⅔ cup of sugar over medium heat. Watch the sugar carefully; it will begin to melt and burn at the edges. This process takes about 5 minutes. When the sugar is entirely caramelized around the perimeter, begin swirling the pan to moisten the rest of the sugar. Slowly add the hot milk. The caramel will seize and solidify. Stir the mixture over medium heat and the caramel will once again turn liquid. The mixture is ready when the caramel is entirely liquefied. Set it aside.

In a small bowl, combine the flour, the remaining ½ cup of sugar, and the salt, and mix with a whisk. Return the caramel to medium heat. Slowly add the flour mixture to the caramel mixture, whisking as you add it. Continue whisking the mixture until it thickens and reaches the consistency of a loose pudding. Remove the pan from the heat.

In a small bowl, slowly add about ½ cup of the hot caramel mixture to the egg yolks, stirring as you do so. Pour the tempered yolks into the remaining hot caramel mixture, stir, and return the pan to the stove. Cook the mixture over medium heat, stirring constantly, for 3 to 5 minutes, until it reaches a stiffer, more custardlike consistency or comes to a boil.

Remove the custard from the heat, and pour it through a sieve into a medium-size bowl to strain out any solids. Stir in the vanilla. Lay a sheet of plastic wrap directly on the surface of the custard to prevent a skin from forming. Allow the custard to cool slightly. When the custard feels warm to the touch, pour it into the prepared crust. Let the pie cool to room temperature, and then refrigerate it. The pie will keep for a day up to this point.

Make the meringue: Preheat the oven to 350°F.

Using an electric mixer on high speed, beat the egg whites with the cream of tartar until frothy. Add the salt and continue beating. As the egg whites turn glossy, slowly add the sugar, 1 tablespoon at a time, incorporating each spoonful before adding the next. Continue to beat until the egg whites reach stiff peaks but are not absolutely dry, about 4 minutes.

Fold in the vanilla.

Spoon some of the meringue around the perimeter of the pie. Spread it until it touches the inner edge of the crust. (It is important to create a seal between the meringue and the crust, to protect against shrinkage.) Mound the rest of the meringue in the center, and then spread it out to meet the meringue along the perimeter. The meringue should cover the entire top of the pie.

Bake the pie for 10 to 15 minutes, until the meringue is golden brown. Remove it from the oven and let it cool to room temperature before enjoying.

Persimmon Pie

For more than sixty-five years, Mitchell, Indiana, has been the home of the Persimmon Festival, a celebration of the indigenous American variety of the fruit that grows wild in southern Indiana. Every September, the town throws a party to welcome the arrival of the persimmons, holding persimmon-centric bake-offs and cook-offs, culminating in the Persimmon Pudding Contest.

Dymple Green, a Mitchell native, is the unofficial queen of the festival and all things persimmon. In the late 1960s she and her husband developed a method for commercially canning persimmon pulp. They called the canned persimmon "Dymple's Delight" and shipped it throughout the United States. Though Dymple's days as the doyenne of canned persimmon are long behind her, she still sells frozen persimmon pulp locally. All you need to do is knock on her back door and ask if she has any left.

This recipe for persimmon pie has been adapted from a slim, photocopied book that Dymple compiled over her years of working at the Persimmon Festival. It is for a dense custard pie, similar in appearance to a pumpkin pie, but with a taste all its own. Delicate and sweet in flavor, the slightly gritty pulp lends the pie a pleasing earthiness.

½ recipe Standard Pie Dough (page 28)

2 large eggs
1½ cups persimmon pulp (see Note)

Note:
To make persimmon pulp, peel very soft, fully ripe American or Hachiya persimmons, and pulse the fruit in a blender or food processor until smooth. About 5 Hachiya persimmons make 1½ cups of pulp.

1 cup whole milk
1 teaspoon vanilla extract
½ cup sugar
Pinch of kosher salt
1 tablespoon cornstarch

Preheat the oven to 375°F.

On a well-floured surface, roll out the dough until it is about ⅛-inch thick and will fit a 9-inch pie plate. Gently pick up the dough, center it over the pie plate, and ease it into the plate. Trim the edges of the dough to leave a 1-inch overhang. Fold the edges under, and then decoratively crimp the perimeter. Return the pie shell to the refrigerator to chill until the filling is ready.

In a medium-size bowl, combine the eggs, persimmon pulp, milk, and vanilla, and stir thoroughly.

In a small bowl, combine the sugar, salt, and cornstarch, and stir to mix well. Add the sugar mixture to the persimmon mixture, and stir well to combine.

Remove the pie shell from the refrigerator, and pour the filling into the shell, spreading it out evenly. Bake the pie for 45 to 50 minutes, until it is golden brown and moderately puffed, and jiggles only slightly when shaken. Remove the pie from the oven, and let it cool to room temperature before enjoying.

PERSIMMONS

Two varieties of persimmons, both originally from Asia, dominate the American market: the Fuyu and the Hachiya. The tomato-shaped Fuyu persimmon is delicious when firm, while the larger, heart-shaped Hachiya must be fully ripe and completely soft before it is consumed. The American persimmon is no larger than a plum, and like the Hachiya, it must be completely ripe and soft before you can eat it. When ripe, persimmons have a flavor similar to a date, perfumed and honeyed. Underripe Hachiya and American persimmons are incredibly astringent, leaving an unpleasant puckering sensation in the mouth.

165

Lemon Pie-Cake

This pie is a classic of the 1950s. Read any Midwestern community cookbook from the era and you're almost certain to find a version in its pages, usually named after the baker who would like to take credit for it: Peg's Lemon Pie-Cake, Shirley's Lemon Pie-Cake, Susan's Lemon Pie-Cake . . . And no wonder. This fluffy, lemony beauty is all about the mysterious alchemy of baking. Simple to prepare—you just separate some eggs, mix the rest of the ingredients, then fold in the beaten egg whites—the real magic takes place in the oven. As the pie bakes, the egg whites rise to the top, creating a sponge-cake-like top layer, while the yolks sink to the bottom, settling into a glorious lemon curd.

I've brought the pie-cake into the twenty-first century with a few strategic updates. To brighten the pie, I increased the amount of lemon zest and decreased the sugar. And while most of the original recipes called for milk, I substituted buttermilk. I love the rich tanginess it offers. This pie is definitely an oldie but a goody; mix one up and let the reveling begin!

½ recipe Standard Pie Dough (page 28) or Rich and
  Buttery Pie Dough (page 30)

2 teaspoons grated lemon zest (from 1 lemon)
¼ cup lemon juice (from approximately 2 lemons)
2 tablespoons unsalted butter, melted and cooled
2 tablespoons all-purpose flour

¾ cup sugar

Pinch of kosher salt

2 large eggs, separated

1 cup buttermilk

Preheat the oven to 375°F.

On a well-floured surface, roll out the dough until it is about ⅛-inch thick and will fit a 9-inch pie plate. Gently pick up the dough, center it over the pie plate, and ease it into the plate. Trim the edges of the dough to leave a 1-inch overhang. Fold the edges under, and then decoratively crimp the perimeter. Return the pie shell to the refrigerator to chill until the filling is ready.

In a medium-size bowl, combine the lemon zest, lemon juice, and melted butter, and stir to mix. In a small bowl, combine the flour, sugar, and salt and stir to mix. Add the sugar mixture to the lemon mixture, and stir well. Set aside.

Using a whisk, beat the egg yolks in a small bowl. Add the buttermilk and whisk until combined. Add the buttermilk mixture to the lemon mixture, and set it aside.

With an electric mixer on high speed, beat the egg whites until they are glossy and stiff but not dry. Gently fold the whites into the lemon-buttermilk mixture until just combined.

Remove the pie shell from the refrigerator, and pour the filling into the shell. Bake the pie for 10 minutes. Then reduce the heat to 350° and continue baking for another 25 to 30 minutes, until the filling is lightly browned and still has some movement when you jiggle the pie plate. Remove the pie from the oven, and let it cool to room temperature before enjoying.

Rhubarb (Pie Plant) Pie

Rhubarb, which is technically a vegetable, is so tart that without the addition of sugar, many people find it inedible. In fact, its leaves actually are *toxic. Since its first cultivation in the United States in the early 1800s (though apocryphal history has it that Benjamin Franklin introduced the native Chinese plant by bringing the seeds to the East Coast in 1772), just what to do besides make a pie with this vegetable-cum-fruit has so puzzled cooks that rhubarb came to be known colloquially as "pie plant."*

Rhubarb is a hardy plant that grows well even in extremely cold climates. Because of this, it is grown in abundance throughout the Midwest, where many of the best "pie plant" pie recipes hail from. Because rhubarb is so astringent, many of the recipes are laden with sugar. But I've always found rhubarb's tartness pleasing—like taking a bite from a crisp-tart apple. My recipe for this traditional double-crusted pie is still sweet, but not cloyingly so— the perfect entrance to spring.

1 recipe Standard Pie Dough (page 28) or
   Rich and Buttery Pie Dough (page 30)

1 pound rhubarb, cut into ¼-inch-thick slices (4 cups)
1¼ cups sugar
¼ cup all-purpose flour
½ teaspoon grated orange zest
⅛ teaspoon ground nutmeg, preferably freshly grated
   (see page 155)

Pinch of kosher salt
2 tablespoons unsalted butter, cut into ¼-inch cubes

Optional
1 tablespoon heavy cream
1 tablespoon turbinado or sanding sugar

Preheat the oven to 425°F.

In a large mixing bowl, combine the rhubarb, sugar, flour, orange zest, nutmeg, and salt, and toss well to coat.

On a well-floured surface, roll out one portion of the dough until it is about ⅛-inch thick and will fit a 9-inch pie plate. Gently pick up the dough, center it over the pie plate, and ease it into the plate. Let the excess dough hang over the rim. Pour in the rhubarb filling, and shake the pie plate gently to spread it out evenly. Dot the surface of the filling with the butter.

Roll out the second portion of dough to the same size. Lay the dough over the filling. Trim the edges of both layers of dough to leave a 1-inch overhang. Pressing the edges together, fold them under, and then decoratively crimp the perimeter. With a sharp knife, cut 5 vents in the top crust.

Bake the pie for 15 minutes. Then reduce the heat to 375° and continue baking for another 40 to 45 minutes, until the crust is golden brown. Allow the pie to cool to room temperature before enjoying.

Optional:
For a lovely sheen on the baked pie, use a pastry brush to paint the surface with the cream. If you like, sprinkle the sugar over the cream. As the pie bakes, the sugar will caramelize, and it will crackle when you slice a wedge of the freshly baked pie.

Browned Butter Butterscotch Meringue Pie

Simple butterscotch—made with milk, brown sugar, and, of course, butter—is delicious enough all on its own. But the butterscotch in this indulgent pie is made even more sumptuous with the addition of brown butter. Brown butter has been enjoying a culinary resurgence for a couple of decades; chefs have been coating butternut squash ravioli with brown butter and sautéing vegetables in this smooth sauce. But the editors of Farm Journal's Complete Pie Cookbook *were on to this delicious ingredient much earlier. Published in 1965, their recipe recommends melting and then browning tablespoons of butter to create a nutty base for this rich pudding. I am glad that it did!*

The pudding all on its own is truly a treat, and so delicious you may want to eat it as is—but exercise some restraint and you will be rewarded. Spoon it over a slightly salty, crisp, and crumbly graham cracker crust, and mound it with a meringue topping, and you will have a pie that is sure to become a favorite.

1 Graham Cracker Crust (page 42)

For the pudding
6 tablespoons (¾ stick) unsalted butter
¾ cup brown sugar
½ teaspoon kosher salt
2 cups whole milk
2 tablespoons all-purpose flour

2 tablespoons cornstarch
3 large egg yolks

For the meringue
3 large egg whites, at room temperature
¼ teaspoon cream of tartar
Pinch of kosher salt
6 tablespoons sugar
½ teaspoon vanilla extract

Make the pudding: Melt the butter in a medium-size stainless-steel or other light-colored saucepan (you'll need to be able to really see the color of the butter as it cooks) over medium heat. The butter will begin to foam, and then the foam will subside. Continue to cook, swirling the pan and keeping a close eye on its contents. The butter will begin to color and become highly aromatic. Watch it closely. When it turns a light nut-brown color, add the brown sugar and the salt, stirring until both are completely incorporated. Remove the pan from the heat.

Slowly pour the milk into the brown butter mixture, stirring as you do so. If the mixture begins to seize, sticking to the pan as you add the milk, simply return the saucepan to medium heat and cook until the mixture melts again.

Combine the flour, cornstarch, and egg yolks in the top of a double boiler. Slowly add the brown butter mixture, whisking constantly to incorporate the ingredients smoothly. Place the pan over simmering water and cook, whisking the contents constantly, for about 8 minutes, until the mixture reaches the consistency of a loose pudding and coats the back of a spoon. Remove the pan from the heat and pour the pudding into the

171

prepared graham cracker crust (the pudding will continue to thicken as it cools). Lay a piece of plastic wrap directly on the surface of the filling to prevent a skin from forming, and refrigerate the pie until the meringue is ready.

Make the meringue: Preheat the oven to 350°F.

Using an electric mixer on high speed, beat the egg whites with the cream of tartar until frothy. Add the salt and continue beating. As the egg whites turn glossy, slowly add the sugar, 1 tablespoon at a time, incorporating each spoonful before adding the next. Continue to beat until the whites reach stiff peaks but are not absolutely dry, about 4 minutes. Fold in the vanilla.

Spoon some of the meringue around the perimeter of the pie. Spread it until it touches the inner edge of the crust. (It is important to create a seal between the meringue and the crust, to protect against shrinkage.) Mound the rest of the meringue in the center, and then spread it out to meet the meringue along the perimeter. The meringue should cover the entire top of the pie.

Bake the pie for 10 to 15 minutes, until the meringue is golden brown. Remove the pie from the oven and allow it to cool to room temperature before enjoying.

Chocolate Cream Pie

Chocolate cream pie is one of those desserts you can make entirely from ready-made store-bought ingredients. A frozen pie crust, a box of instant pudding mix, a large tub of whipped topping, and voilà—dessert is ready! The resulting pie may even be delicious, much in the same way that a box of mac 'n' cheese, with its packet of neon dehydrated cheese, is—it holds a soft spot in your heart but leaves a hard lump in your stomach. But let me tell you, dessert can be better—infinitely better!

Taken on their own, there's nothing special about the ingredients that make up this pie, but together they are magic. The crumbly vanilla wafer crust is salty-sweet. The chocolate pudding, made with both unsweetened cocoa powder and semisweet chocolate, brings depth and complexity. Real whipped cream, silky and ethereal, ties it all together. Garnish with chocolate curls, if desired. One bite and you'll be sold. You won't even miss all of those boxes—though your recycling bin might.

1 Vanilla Wafer Crust (page 43)

For the filling
¼ cup unsweetened cocoa powder
½ cup sugar
2 tablespoons cornstarch
1 tablespoon all-purpose flour
¼ teaspoon kosher salt
2 cups whole milk

Note:

The chocolate filling calls for 3 egg yolks. Instead of tossing the whites (if you don't have another use for them), you could serve this pie with a meringue topping in place of the whipped cream. Simply omit the whipped cream and follow the recipe for any one of the meringue toppings in this chapter.

3 large egg yolks
2 ounces semisweet chocolate, chopped
2 tablespoons unsalted butter
1 teaspoon vanilla extract

For the topping
1 cup heavy cream
3 tablespoons confectioners' sugar

Combine the cocoa powder, sugar, cornstarch, flour, salt, and 1 cup of the milk in a medium-size saucepan and whisk until fairly smooth. Add the egg yolks and the remaining 1 cup milk, and whisk to incorporate.

Place the saucepan over medium heat, and whisking constantly, bring the mixture to a boil. As soon as it reaches a boil, remove the pan from the heat. The mixture should have thickened to a puddinglike consistency that is still somewhat runny. (It will thicken considerably as it cools.)

Pour the pudding into a heatproof bowl. Add the chocolate, butter, and vanilla, and stir until the chocolate has melted. Lay a piece of plastic wrap directly on the surface of the pudding to prevent a skin from forming, and allow it to cool to room temperature. The filling can be prepared up to 1 day in advance.

Pour the cooled pudding into the prepared crust, and refrigerate the pie until you're ready to make the whipped cream.

Just before you're ready to serve the pie, remove it from the refrigerator. In a medium-size bowl, combine the cream and the confectioners' sugar, and using an electric mixer, whip the cream until it forms soft peaks. Mound the whipped cream on top of the pudding, and serve.

PIES of the WEST

If you're a locavore, living in the West is

as easy as pie. The West Coast has a moderate year-round climate, so there's always *something* in season. It's no surprise that many of the West's winning pies are produce-driven. Washington State alone grows 60 percent of all the apples eaten in the United States, Oregon and Washington grow 80 percent of the pears, and California grows nearly 70 percent of all the strawberries, grapes, peaches, and nectarines in this country. The region is fertile to say the least.

California is the source of more unusual fruit as well. The Coachella Valley produces sweet-as-candy dates; smooth, thin-skinned, and fragrant Meyer lemons grow in backyards throughout the state; and finger-staining olallieberries bud in the fog along the coast near Half Moon Bay. Sweet-tart olallieberries are a hybrid of a hybrid, a crossbreeding of the loganberry and the youngberry, each of which is itself a cross between a blackberry and another berry. In the loganberry's case it's a raspberry, and in the youngberry's case it's a dewberry. Got that? In the universe of berries, olallieberries are still in their infancy—they were developed in 1935 at Oregon State University in cooperation with the USDA Agricultural Research Service. Oddly, olallieberries never really took off in their native state, but they flourish in California, where they're grown in abundance during a fairly short summer season.

Olallieberries are delicious fresh off the vine, but the purple, staining berry makes an exemplary pie. For the best slice of olallieberry pie—besides the one you make yourself—you'll want to head straight to Duarte's Tavern in Pescadero, California. Duarte's is a big restaurant in a little town. If you weren't looking for Pescadero, it would be easy to miss entirely. Located two miles off Highway 1—the scenic ocean highway that runs from Orange County to Mendocino—and fifteen miles south of the relative hustle and bustle of Half Moon Bay, its downtown is just two blocks long, with no sidewalks to speak of. Breathe in deeply, and you can smell the ocean, taste the salt in the air. Smack in the middle of downtown stands this family-owned restaurant that's been in business for more than one hundred years, since its first incarnation as a bar serving ten-cent whiskeys.

Today Duarte's is considered a landmark—it was even awarded "American Classic" status by the James Beard Foundation, one of only five restaurants in the United States that has received the honor. One might think of a tavern as dark, smoky, and forbidding, but Duarte's is anything but. Bright and bustling, with honey-colored wood-paneled walls and blond wood floors, it's more chalet than speakeasy. I arrived at Duarte's on a Friday just before noon. Kathy Duarte and her brother, Tim, are the fourth generation of Duartes running the tavern. Although the lunch rush was starting, Kathy met me with a warm handshake and a smile. The inner workings of the restaurant are an open book, so I was shuttled back into the kitchen. Together we headed straight for the pie-making station.

Kathy described the unusual dough they use for their crusts. The recipe comes from Emma Duarte, Tim and Kathy's grandmother, who was responsible for expanding the tavern into a full-fledged restaurant back in the 1930s, and it is clear that this is not your typical pie dough. Peeking into the large stainless-steel bowl sitting on the counter, I saw a soft yet crumbly mess of flour and shortening. The shaggy mixture had large bits of shortening in it, the size of olallieberries themselves. The concoction looked more like biscuit dough than any pie dough I had seen. The baker reached into the bowl—there was nothing delicate about her handling—and scooped a mass of the mixture onto a very well-floured board. She then reached for one of the half-gallon containers of milk on the counter and sloshed a generous splash of it on the ragged mass, kneading quickly and forming a smooth ball of dough. She rolled the dough into a rough circle, thicker than I expected, and slipped it into an 8-inch pie plate. No refrigeration. Nothing automated. Just a few simple ingredients. The whole process took about thirty seconds. It was clear that this baker had made more than a few pies in her lifetime. This relaxed, no-nonsense attitude is something we can all aspire to in our crust-making endeavors!

Kathy told me that all the berries Duarte's uses are flash-frozen, even at the height of the season. "That way we can guarantee the same quality, no matter what season you come to eat at the restaurant," she explained. I was dumbfounded when Kathy mentioned that Duarte's goes through thirty thousand pounds of olallieberries in a year just to bake those luscious pies. When Emma Duarte first started making the pies, all the berries were grown by Kathy and Tim's grandfather in a garden behind the restaurant. Now they purchase anywhere from three to four thousand pounds of the fruit from a local Pescadero farm and contract with a farm just a few hours away in Watsonville for the rest.

Piled in a restaurant pan in the kitchen was a mass of olallieberries—at least enough for a half dozen pies—soaking in a pool of their own juice. The baker slid the pan into a warm oven to thaw the berries, which yielded a sort of berry stew. She then strained the berries of their juice (which the kitchen reserves for sauce or vinaigrette) and scooped the berries into a bowl. She spooned out a cup of sugar, took a large handful of flour, and added both to the bowl, mixing quickly. The berries got a thorough bashing with her metal spoon before she poured them into the pie shell. She rolled out a round of dough to top the pie. There was no crimping, no fluting; she simply folded the remnants of dough underneath itself. Lastly, she vented the pie with a skewer and popped it in the oven. And that was it—no butter cubed and placed under the final crust, no lemon zest mingling with the olallieberries, no spoonful of cinnamon, no splash of vanilla extract.

At the end of my kitchen tour, I took a seat at one of the unembellished tables in the dining room and ordered—what else—a slice of olallieberry pie. Before digging in, I paused for a moment, fork poised in midair. The slice in front of me was unadorned and rough-hewn, clearly handmade. I plunged my fork in. The crust was flaky and resilient. Deeply pigmented juice flooded my plate. I took a bite. The flavor was intense—snappy fruit tempered by just the right amount of sugar. My mouth crackled with berry seeds. As I took another bite, I seemed to be communing with a little piece of a Northern California coastal summer day. The cool sea fog there burns off by afternoon, giving way to the California sun, and this rustic pie, unmarred by extraneous flavors, captured it all: its simplicity, its ease, its pleasure. If *you* are ever craving a taste of California summer, don't forget: Duarte's has a slice of olallieberry pie waiting. Or you could make your own.

Olallieberry Pie

In the mid-1970s, Ron Duarte, the third-generation owner of Duarte's Tavern in Pescadero, California, began planting olallieberry bushes in the sizable fruit and vegetable garden behind the restaurant. Thanks to the temperate climate and gentle sea breezes, the bushes flourished, and soon his mother began to make pies with their glut of berries. And the now-famous Duarte's Olallieberry Pie was born.

I know that many of you do not have access to olallieberries. That's quite all right; this pie is equally delicious made with a combination of blackberries and raspberries. It's my homage to the Duarte's pie—dark, sweet, a little bit gritty due to the berry seeds, and altogether delicious. If you choose to make this pie with frozen berries in the wintertime, just make sure that the berries are com- pletely *thawed, and reserve the juice for another use.*

1 recipe Standard Pie Dough (page 28)

1½ pounds (6 cups) olallieberries, or 1 pound (4 cups) blackberries and 10 ounces (2 cups) raspberries
1 cup sugar
¼ cup all-purpose flour
Pinch of kosher salt

Optional
1 tablespoon heavy cream
1 tablespoon turbinado or sanding sugar

Rinse the berries, spread them out in a single layer on paper-towel-lined cookie sheets, and allow them to dry completely.

Preheat the oven to 425°F.

In a large bowl, gently toss the berries with the sugar, flour, and salt until thoroughly mixed. Set aside.

On a well-floured surface, roll out one portion of the dough until it is about ⅛-inch thick and will fit a 9-inch pie plate. Gently pick up the dough, center it over the pie plate, and ease it into the plate. Let the excess dough hang over the rim. Pour in the filling and shake the pie plate gently to spread it out evenly.

Roll out the second portion of dough to the same size. Lay the dough over the filling. Trim the edges of both layers of dough to leave a 1-inch overhang. Pressing the edges together, fold them under, and then decoratively crimp the perimeter. With a sharp knife, cut 5 vents in the top crust.

Bake the pie for 15 minutes. Then reduce the heat to 375° and continue baking for 35 to 40 minutes, until the crust is golden brown. Let the pie cool to room temperature before enjoying.

Optional:
For a lovely sheen on the baked pie, use a pastry brush to paint the surface with the cream. If you like, sprinkle the sugar over the cream. As the pie bakes, the sugar will caramelize, and it will crackle when you slice a wedge of the freshly baked pie.

Apricot-Ginger Pie

Come late spring, I am more than ready to say farewell to my overcoat. And just when the wintertime blahs become too much for me to bear, apricots hit the markets, signaling the welcome arrival of warmer months. In California, apricots are the early risers of the new season, and they always will be one of my favorite fruits. Wonderfully sweet, they loosely grasp their stones, perfume the air, and, with their soft, rosy skins, are a feast for the eyes as well.

However, good apricots can be hard to come by. To reduce bruising during travel, commercial growers often pick the fruit before it's fully ripe, while it's still firm. Underripe apricots are bland and uninspiring. While an unripe apricot will soften and become juicier sitting on your counter, it will not become sweeter or more flavorful once separated from the mother tree. But if you live near a farmers' market, or are luckier still and have access to an apricot tree yourself, take advantage of the short season and make a pie. The fruit becomes more concentrated upon baking, so if you are dealing with less-than-perfect specimens, don't worry—their flavor will only sweeten and intensify. The addition of candied ginger gives this pie a spicy, modern taste.

1 recipe Standard Pie Dough (page 28) or
   Cornmeal Pie Dough (page 38)

1 pound 10 ounces apricots (about 15 apricots), pitted
   and quartered

1 tablespoon finely diced candied ginger

2 tablespoons all-purpose flour

2 tablespoons cornstarch

¾ cup sugar

Juice of 1 small lemon

Pinch of kosher salt

Optional

1 tablespoon heavy cream

1 tablespoon turbinado or sanding sugar

Preheat the oven to 425°F.

In a large bowl, combine the apricots, candied ginger, flour, cornstarch, sugar, lemon juice, and salt, and toss gently to mix. Set aside.

On a well-floured surface, roll out one portion of the dough until it is about ⅛-inch thick and will fit a 9-inch pie plate. Gently pick up the dough, center it over the pie plate, and ease it into the plate. Let the excess dough hang over the rim. Pour in the filling and shake the pie plate gently to spread it out evenly.

Roll out the second portion of dough to the same size. Lay the dough over the filling. Trim the edges of both layers of dough to leave a 1-inch overhang. Pressing the edges together, fold them under, and then decoratively crimp the perimeter. With a sharp knife, cut 5 vents in the top crust.

Bake the pie for 15 minutes. Then reduce the heat to 375° and continue baking for 35 to 40 minutes, until the crust is golden brown. Let the pie cool to room temperature before enjoying.

Optional:
For a lovely sheen on the baked pie, use a pastry brush to paint the surface with the cream. If you like, sprinkle the sugar over the cream. As the pie bakes, the sugar will caramelize, and it will crackle when you slice a wedge of the freshly baked pie.

185

Raspberry Custard Pie with Streusel Topping

On the bramble, raspberries grow furiously and rapidly. The bushes quickly multiply, and during the summer months, it seems like a berry explosion! But raspberries are delicate—hardy on the bush but frail off—making them almost *too difficult to make a pie out of all on their own. Almost. This pie takes advantage of the copious amount of berries available at the peak of the summer season. Once you get hold of some raspberries, make this pie quickly— the berries don't have much of a shelf life. The silky, not-too-sweet custard lets the subtleties of the raspberries shine through. The berries hold their shape within the custard filling, lending substance to the pie, and the simple streusel topping—just flour, sugar, and butter—bakes into a crisp, sweet shell. The pie is great for dessert, but it makes a wonderful breakfast as well.*

½ recipe Standard Pie Dough (page 28)

For the filling
12 ounces (3 cups) raspberries
½ cup plain yogurt (low-fat or full-fat)
3 large eggs
½ cup sugar
¼ cup all-purpose flour
1 teaspoon vanilla extract

For the streusel topping
½ cup all-purpose flour
½ cup brown sugar

4 tablespoons (½ stick) unsalted butter, melted
Pinch of kosher salt

Rinse the berries, spread them out in a single layer on paper-towel-lined cookie sheets, and allow them to dry completely.

Preheat the oven to 400°F.

On a well-floured surface, roll out the dough until it is about ⅛-inch thick and will fit a 9-inch pie plate. Gently pick up the dough, center it over the pie plate, and ease it into the plate. Trim the edges of the dough to leave a 1-inch overhang. Fold the edges under, and then decoratively crimp the perimeter.

Make the filling: Spread the raspberries evenly over the bottom of the prepared pie shell. Set aside.

In a medium-size bowl, whisk together the yogurt and the eggs until smooth. Add the sugar, flour, and vanilla, and continue to beat until incorporated. Pour the custard mixture evenly over the raspberries; it should just cover the berries. Set aside.

Make the streusel: In a small bowl, mix together the flour, brown sugar, melted butter, and salt. Sprinkle the streusel evenly over the raspberry filling.

Bake the pie for 35 to 40 minutes, until the streusel is golden brown and has melted a bit. Remove the pie from the oven and let it cool to room temperature before enjoying.

Breakfast Apple Pie

I love pie for breakfast. In my family, we've been eating pie for breakfast for as long as we've been eating pie. A little fruit, some carbohydrates from the crust, protein from the butter, and there you have it—a perfectly balanced meal!

This pie is a take on Marion Cunningham's Breakfast Apple Pie. For years, Marion Cunningham was James Beard's right-hand woman, assisting him in teaching cooking courses throughout the country and then returning to her home in the San Francisco Bay Area. In 1990 she became Fannie Farmer, revising the acclaimed cookbook. To top it all off, she has written cookbooks under her own moniker as well. Her genius cookbook, The Breakfast Book, *is a classic. In it, her apple pie recipe features a cornflake filling and a streusel top. The cornflakes act as a bed for a layer of delicately spiced sliced apples. As the pie bakes, the flakes lose their crunch and become a thickener for the apples, absorbing the juice they release as they cook.*

Marion Cunningham is a living legend, the grande dame of American home cooking and probably a certifiable pie expert. Her breakfast apple pie is delicious, moist, and hearty. But I've never been one to leave well enough alone. In my version, I remove the cornflakes from the filling and add them to the streusel topping. The smashed flakes make the streusel extra crunchy and preserve the flavor of the cereal. I then make a custard of sorts and add it to the apple filling. Once baked, it is light and creamy—just like scrambled eggs. Make sure to use tart apples, such as Granny Smiths or Pippins—nothing too sweet. After all, this pie is for breakfast!

½ recipe Standard Pie Dough (page 28)

For the filling
14 ounces (about 2 medium) tart baking apples, such as Granny Smith or Pippin, cored, peeled, and cut into ¼-inch-thick slices (3 cups)

½ cup sugar

½ teaspoon ground cinnamon

Pinch of kosher salt

3 large eggs

1 tablespoon all-purpose flour

1 cup whole milk

1 teaspoon vanilla extract

For the streusel topping
¼ cup all-purpose flour

¼ cup brown sugar

½ cup cornflakes

Pinch of kosher salt

4 tablespoons (½ stick) unsalted butter, chilled, cut into ½-inch cubes

Preheat the oven to 325°F.

On a well-floured surface, roll out the dough until it is about ⅛-inch thick and will fit a 9-inch pie plate. Gently pick up the dough, center it over the pie plate, and ease it into the plate. Trim the edges of the dough to leave a 1-inch overhang. Fold the edges under, and then decoratively crimp the perimeter. Return the pie shell to the refrigerator to chill until the filling is ready.

In a large mixing bowl, toss the apples, sugar, cinnamon, and salt until well mixed.

Remove the pie shell from the refrigerator. Pour the apple filling into the shell, shaking the pie plate gently to distribute it evenly. Set aside.

In a medium-size bowl, lightly beat the eggs. Add the flour, milk, and vanilla, and beat until smooth. Pour the egg mixture over the apples. Bake the pie for 35 minutes.

Make the streusel: Meanwhile, in a small bowl, mix together the flour, brown sugar, cornflakes, and salt. Crush the cornflakes with your hands until they are about the size of raw oats. Add the butter, and continue to mix with your hands, rubbing the butter between your fingers until you have a crumbly streusel.

When the pie has baked for 35 minutes, remove it from the oven and gently pat the streusel over the filling. (The custard will not be set at this time.) Return the pie to the oven, and continue baking for about 40 more minutes, until the streusel has melted slightly into the custard and the cornflakes are crispy and brown. Let the pie cool to room temperature before enjoying.

Date Pie

You may think of Southern California as the land of beaches, movie stars, and billboards, but it is also date country. Sweet, honeyed dates grow in abundance here, thanks to the arid climate and warm weather. The weather in SoCal is similar to the Mediterranean regions of the Middle East, where people have prized this fruit's candylike taste and long shelf life for six thousand years.

If you are munching on a date in this country, chances are it came from the Coachella Valley, not far from the resorts and golf courses of Palm Springs. In Coachella, spiky fronds of date palms heavy with fruit punctuate the skyline. Farm stands sell everything from date rolls, to date shakes made of ice cream blended with date crystals. If you're really lucky, you may even find a slice or two of date pie.

My date pie is sweet, with a chewy bite from the pieces of chopped fruit. A bit of tangy sour cream tempers the candied flavor of the dates, and the sweetened coconut that tops the pie lends it an almost tropical feel. It is the perfect dessert to make in the dead of winter while dreaming of that warm California sun.

½ recipe Standard Pie Dough (page 28)

⅓ cup sour cream
½ cup whole milk
½ cup dark brown sugar
½ cup sugar

There are almost as many varieties of dates as there are varieties of apples, but in this country, two dates dominate the market: Deglet Noor and Medjool. Deglet Noor dates have an almost translucent tawny flesh, a chewy texture, and a mildly sweet flavor. Medjool dates have a meatier flesh, a deeper tone, and a rich, sweet flavor. Because of their soft, sumptuous nature, Medjool dates are ideal for baking; they almost melt away, leaving behind a butterscotchy flavor. If you have trouble finding Medjool dates, though, go ahead and use the more widely available Deglet Noor variety. Your pie will still be delicious, with a smoothly sweet, nutty flavor.

2 tablespoons unsalted butter, melted

2 large eggs

1 teaspoon vanilla extract

Pinch of kosher salt

¾ cup chopped dates

1 tablespoon all-purpose flour

⅓ cup sweetened shredded coconut

Preheat the oven to 425°F.

On a well-floured surface, roll out the dough until it is about ⅛-inch thick and will fit a 9-inch pie plate. Gently pick up the dough, center it over the pie plate, and ease it into the plate. Trim the edges of the dough to leave a 1-inch overhang. Fold the edges under, and then decoratively crimp the perimeter. Return the pie shell to the refrigerator to chill until the filling is ready.

In a medium-size bowl, whisk together the sour cream, milk, sugars, melted butter, eggs, vanilla, and salt until blended. In a small bowl, toss the date pieces with the flour until evenly coated. Add the dates to the custard mixture, stirring gently.

Remove the pie shell from the refrigerator. Pour in the filling and shake the pie plate gently to distribute it evenly.

Bake the pie for 10 minutes. Then reduce the heat to 375° and continue baking for another 20 minutes. Remove the pie from the oven and sprinkle the coconut evenly over the top. Return the pie to the oven and bake for another 10 to 15 minutes, until the coconut is browned and the custard is almost completely set. Remove the pie from the oven. Serve at room temperature or slightly warm.

Black Bottom Pie

The black bottom pie is a dreamy confection—the type of heirloom dessert that tastes of the time and effort its baker took composing a thing of such sweet beauty. Essentially it is a chiffon pie, a lighter-than-air pie made with beaten egg whites and stabilized with gelatin. A crumbly gingersnap or graham cracker crust anchors the creamy fillings: a rich chocolate pudding topped with a layer of eggnoglike vanilla custard tinged with dark rum. This pie is a bit of a time commitment, and it does require dirtying a few dishes, but each step is relatively easy to complete. And I assure you, one taste and you will understand what the fuss has been about for nearly a century. If you'd like to take this pie all the way over the top, garnish it with a layer of sweetened whipped cream. A sprinkling of chocolate curls always adds a nice touch.

1 Gingersnap Crust (page 44) or
   Graham Cracker Crust (page 42)

1 envelope (¼ ounce) unflavored gelatin
2 cups whole milk
4 large eggs, separated
1 tablespoon cornstarch
1 cup sugar
⅛ teaspoon kosher salt, plus a pinch extra
2 ounces semisweet or bittersweet chocolate, chopped
3 tablespoons dark rum

¼ teaspoon cream of tartar

1 teaspoon vanilla extract

In a small bowl, dissolve the gelatin in ¼ cup of cold water. Set aside.

In a medium-size saucepan, heat the milk until it's just simmering.

In the top of a double boiler, beat the egg yolks, cornstarch, ½ cup of the sugar, and the ⅛ teaspoon of salt. Slowly add the hot milk to the mixture, beating until the mixture is smooth. Place the pan over simmering water, and whisk constantly until the custard has the consistency of a loose pudding and coats the back of a spoon, about 8 minutes. Remove the pan from the heat, add the softened gelatin, and stir well.

In a small bowl, combine 1 cup of the custard with the chopped chocolate, stirring until the chocolate melts completely. Pour the chocolate custard into the prepared crust, and refrigerate until cool.

Meanwhile, in a small bowl, combine the remaining custard with the rum, and stir to blend. Cover, and refrigerate until the custard reaches room temperature, about 45 minutes. At this point, the custard should still be fairly loose.

When the rum custard is cool, combine the egg whites and the cream of tartar in a large bowl, and using an electric mixer on high speed, whip until frothy. Add the pinch of salt, and continue beating. As the whites turn glossy, slowly add the remaining ½ cup of sugar, 1 tablespoon at a time, incorporating each spoonful before adding the next. Continue to beat until the whites form stiff peaks but are not absolutely dry, about 4 minutes. Fold in the vanilla.

Fold the rum custard into the egg whites until completely blended. Remove the partially filled pie shell from the refrigerator. Spoon the rum chiffon custard over the chocolate custard, making sure to cover the chocolate completely. Return the pie to the refrigerator and chill for a minimum of 4 hours, or as long as 8 hours, before serving.

ONE SCREWY-LOOKING PIE

In true American fashion, black bottom pie has been the subject of much mythologizing, in spite of—or perhaps because of—its rather murky history. In his 1972 classic, *American Cookery,* James Beard claims that this pie "began appearing in cookbooks around the turn of the century." Despite his authority, I find Beard's claim suspect—and he didn't cite any sources! Duncan Hines (yes, *that* Duncan Hines, namesake of supermarket cake mixes), a traveling salesman who made his name rating restaurants for travelers in the era before interstate highways, popularized the pie in the 1941 edition of his book, *Adventures in Good Cooking,* in a review of Oklahoma City's Dolores Restaurant—it was one of their signature desserts. But Hines was not the first to write about black bottom pie. In his 1939 book, *Pie Marches On*, Monroe Boston Strause, "Pie King," ingenious self-promoter, and all-around immodest character, claims not only to have invented the pie in the late 1920s but also to have disseminated the recipe throughout the United States. From where did Strause hail? Los Angeles, California, where he was a consultant for the famous Brown Derby restaurant in Hollywood. Another Los Angeles hot spot, the late, lamented, and fabulous Ambassador Hotel, which was home to the famous Cocoanut Grove nightclub, also featured a version of the black bottom pie as a menu staple. So many stories, but just one pie!

The earliest print reference to a black bottom pie appears in 1931, in the local Brownsville, Texas, newspaper. Page three featured a recipe for a chilled pie with two fillings—a chocolate pudding and a lemon pudding. Close, but not exactly the black bottom pie of lore. But a 1933 article in a Van Nuys newspaper (Van Nuys is a neighborhood in Los Angeles) contains a recipe for a double-layered chocolate and vanilla custard pie, made with egg whites stabilized with "Jelatine" and called the black bottom pie. The recipe circulated around the West in the early '30s, appearing in bakery, grocery, and restaurant advertisements. In Reno, Nevada, you could get a whole black bottom pie topped with "Pure Whipped Cream" for a costly 29 cents back in 1932.

By the mid-'30s syndicated newspaper lifestyle columns reporting on black bottom pie began circulating around the country. Housewives began serving the pie at bridge games and social functions. In 1936, the syndicated "Sister Mary" column featured a black bottom pie from Geneva, Wisconsin, with photo included. The year after, a syndicated column by Mrs. Gaynor Maddox describes it as "one screwy-looking pie," attributing its origin to the Brown Derby: "Out there in Hollywood where so many odd things happen," she writes, "this pie turns out to taste more sensible than it looks."

Recipes are ephemeral. They're jotted down on scraps of paper, whispered from ear to ear, clipped from the newspaper. So while we may never know just *who* invented this gorgeous relic of American desserts, all documentary evidence seems to lead back to the West. I tilt my hat to the region; this is one hell of a pie!

Citrus Chiffon Pie

I developed this light, creamy, and refreshing pie in the spirit, if not the letter, of "Pie King" Monroe Boston Strause's famous chiffon pies. Its bright flavor embodies a sunny Los Angeles day. A billowy cloud of egg white chiffon, redolent of oranges and lemons, is mounded in a graham cracker or vanilla wafer crust and popped in the refrigerator to cool. With its delicate filling and crisp crust, this is the type of pie that is deceptively easy to eat, slice after slice.

1 Graham Cracker Crust (page 42) or
   Vanilla Wafer Crust (page 43)

1 envelope (¼ ounce) unflavored gelatin
½ cup plus ⅓ cup sugar
Pinch of kosher salt
4 large eggs, separated (see Note)
⅓ cup lemon juice (from approximately 2 lemons)
½ cup orange juice (from approximately 3 oranges)
½ teaspoon grated lemon zest
1 teaspoon grated orange zest

In a medium-size saucepan, mix together the gelatin, the ½ cup of sugar, and the salt.

In a medium-size bowl, combine the egg yolks, lemon juice, orange juice, and ¼ cup of water. Beat until smooth.

Stir the egg yolk mixture into the gelatin mixture, and bring to a boil over medium heat, dissolving the gelatin and sugar. Remove the saucepan from the heat, transfer the contents to a bowl, cover, and refrigerate until partially set, about 1 hour.

When the gelatin mixture is partially set, add the egg whites to a large bowl, and using an electric mixer on high speed, beat the whites until they form soft peaks. Gradually add the remaining ⅓ cup sugar. Continue to beat the egg whites until they are glossy and firm but not dry. Fold the gelatin mixture into the egg whites, along with the lemon and orange zests.

Mound the mixture in the prepared crust, spreading it out evenly. Refrigerate for a minimum of 4 hours, or as long as 8 hours, before serving.

Note:

I am not sure why, but sadly, chiffon pies have all but been forgotten today. Perhaps it is due to the fact that the egg whites in chiffon pies are uncooked. Because of this, it's important to use the freshest organic eggs possible.

THE PIE ENGINEER
VERSUS
THE HOME BAKER

Monroe Boston Strause was born in Los Angeles around the turn of the twentieth century. At the young age of sixteen, he partnered with his uncle, who was a baker. Strause was a tinkerer, always adding to and embellishing the pies he and his uncle were making, always searching for the "best" way to standardize pies. In many ways his philosophy is in sharp contrast to the philosophy set forth in this book. Strause sought perfection. He had a vision of an America in which every dessert case was filled with beautiful, homogeneous pies that were as much about presentation as they were about flavor. Fruit fillings were precooked, additional cornstarch was used to thicken pies for easier slicing, creams and custards were prepared ahead, chilled for

days, and then spooned into premade shells as needed. Weepy meringues were targeted . . . and eradicated with additional tapioca flour. The idea that a pie can be lopsided, overflowing, and still delectable would have been a ghastly proposition to Strause.

He intended his book, *Pie Marches On*, for use by bakery and restaurant chefs as much as by home bakers, with measurements for making one pie (amateur!), five pies (getting there!), and ten pies (now we're cooking!) at a time. Strause has been called "The King of Pies" and a "Pie Engineer," but it is unclear who actually coined these titles—it was likely Strause himself. As his success as a pie specialist grew, his ego grew right alongside it, in proportion with his towering meringue toppings. Strause traveled the country, advising restaurant chefs and bakers about how they too could produce the perfect pie.

Strause was not a modest man, no eater of humble pie. In a town like Los Angeles, filled with movie stars and entertainment industry executives, this was a man whose calling card was pie. One of the very first pictures in *Pie Marches On* shows Strause presenting an orange chiffon pie to Mary Pickford. Strause towers over Pickford, and the pie is equally larger than life—at least twelve inches in diameter, with a shocking, almost aggressive, crown of stiff white chiffon peaks. Ms. Pickford, a wisp of a thing, is poised, fork in hand, ready to dig into Strause's creation. The caption reads, "Mary Pickford, America's Sweetheart, tastes a delicious orange chiffon pie presented to her by the author." The photograph seems to suggest that Strause is no simple baker, but rather a Svengali of all things sweet, ready to work his nefarious magic through the power of pie.

Though Strause's claim that he invented both the black bottom pie and the Dutch apple pie is up for debate, he *is* likely the inventor of chiffon pies, with many books and bakers citing his responsibility for this voluminous confection. In *Pie Marches On*, when introducing the lemon and orange chiffon pies to readers, Strause states: "These recipes have been imitated by many, but seldom equaled. Don't be fooled by their simplicity because the simplest things often give the best results." He follows this sage advice with a hint of bravado: "So take the doctor's advice in reading the prescription. Read it three times before attempting to fill it."

Avocado Pie

I know you may be wondering . . . Is avocado pie sweet? And the answer is yes. A decadent, silky combination of avocado, lime juice, and sweetened condensed milk, this pie is a delicious throwback to a bygone era in California's history. In the 1950s, recipes for this unique pie began appearing in magazines and were written about in cookbooks. Most people think of the avocado as strictly a vegetable, slicing it on salads or placing a wedge on top of a sandwich. But Californians know better. The avocado is indeed a fruit, and California grows about 90 percent of all the avocados consumed in this country. This pie is smooth, with a luxurious texture and a subtle flavor, but beware—it is rich. No whipped cream required; it really doesn't need it.

1 Graham Cracker Crust (page 42)

2 ripe avocados, peeled and pitted
¼ cup fresh lime juice (from approximately 4 limes)
One 15-ounce can sweetened condensed milk

In a blender, combine the avocados, lime juice, and sweetened condensed milk. Process for 3 to 5 minutes, until the mixture is completely smooth.

Pour the avocado mixture into the prepared crust. Smooth the surface of the pie, cover it with plastic wrap, and refrigerate it for 3 hours. (The lime juice in the mixture will prevent the avocado from browning.)

Serve this rich pie chilled.

Glazed Strawberry-Rhubarb Pie

This is the pie of my youth. My grandmother was a stupendous pie maker. She was one of those women who never used a measuring spoon, who thought that leveling off a cup of flour was ridiculous. She cooked by feel, by touch. She was also a very generous cook. My grandma had six children and fourteen grandchildren, knew every one of our favorite pies, and baked them at each family gathering. Trust me—there were a lot of pies!

My all-time favorite pie was strawberry-rhubarb. When I was growing up, my grandma filled all of my pie-eating desires, but when she passed away, I felt the need to break out the rolling pin. This is my recipe for strawberry-rhubarb pie. You layer the fruit, spooning the sugar over each layer. During the baking process, the sugar melts, creating a glaze that sweetens the pie but maintains the integrity of each piece of fruit. Although she didn't pass this recipe down to me, I still think of my grandma each time I make it.

1 recipe Standard Pie Dough (page 28) or
   Sour Cream Pie Dough (page 36)

1¼ cups sugar
⅓ cup all-purpose flour
½ teaspoon grated orange zest
Pinch of kosher salt
12 ounces rhubarb, sliced into ¼-inch pieces
   (3 cups)

1 pound strawberries, cleaned, hulled, and quartered (3 cups)

2 tablespoons unsalted butter, cut into ½-inch cubes

Optional

1 tablespoon heavy cream

1 tablespoon turbinado or sanding sugar

Preheat the oven to 425°F.

In a small bowl, combine the sugar, flour, orange zest, and salt. Stir well, and set aside.

In a medium-size bowl, toss the rhubarb and the strawberries together. Set aside.

On a well-floured surface, roll out one portion of the dough until it is about ⅛-inch thick and will fit a 9-inch pie plate. Gently pick up the dough, center it over the pie plate, and ease it into the plate. Let the excess dough hang over the rim.

Spread half of the fruit mixture in the pie plate. Sprinkle half of the sugar mixture over the fruit. Repeat the layers of fruit and sugar. Dot the surface with the butter.

Roll out the second portion of dough to the same size. Lay the dough over the filling. Trim the edges of both layers of the dough to leave a 1-inch overhang. Pressing the edges together, fold them under, and then decoratively crimp the perimeter. With a sharp knife, cut 5 vents in the top crust.

Bake the pie for 15 minutes. Then reduce the heat to 375° and continue baking for 45 to 50 minutes, until the crust is golden brown. Let the pie cool to room temperature before enjoying.

Optional:
For a lovely sheen on the baked pie, use a pastry brush to paint the surface with the cream. If you like, sprinkle the sugar over the cream. As the pie bakes, the sugar will caramelize, and it will crackle when you slice a wedge of the freshly baked pie.

Fresh Strawberry Pie

My sister is six years older than I. By the time I was in middle school, she was in college. A few times a year I would spend the weekend with her at UC Davis, about an hour and a half drive from home. My parents would load my overnight bag into their boat of a car, and we'd meet my sister at the halfway point: a Marie Callender's restaurant. The lobby of the restaurant featured a refrigerated case that housed numerous pies. The brightest and glossiest by far was the "fresh" strawberry pie. Whole berries, each one larger than a child's fist and doused in a shocking red glaze, topped the pie. No matter the season—spring or winter—the strawberry pie was always available.

But when I actually ordered a slice of fresh strawberry pie at any chain restaurant, I was always disappointed. The berries were inevitably underripe and crunchy, the glaze tasted slightly medicinal, and the pie lacked the gentle sweetness that I associate with fruit pies. This recipe is the antidote to the sad strawberry pies of my youth. The glaze is made from crushed strawberries; it is clear and pink—not candy-apple red. The berries are quartered, allowing for maximum juiciness. And let's not forget about pure whipped cream. This pie has plenty of that, too!

1 Graham Cracker Crust (page 42)

For the glaze
10 ounces strawberries (about 10 medium berries),
   cleaned and hulled

205

Grated zest and juice of 1 medium lemon
3 tablespoons cornstarch
¾ cup sugar
Pinch of kosher salt

For the filling
12 ounces strawberries, cleaned, hulled, and quartered
  (2 cups)
1 cup heavy cream
2 tablespoons confectioners' sugar
1 teaspoon vanilla extract

Make the glaze: By hand, or with a potato masher, mash the strawberries into a juicy pulp in a bowl. Combine the strawberries, lemon zest and juice, and ½ cup of water in a small saucepan, and warm over medium heat.

In a small bowl, mix the cornstarch, sugar, and salt. Add the cornstarch mixture to the strawberry mixture, raise the heat to high, and bring to a boil, stirring constantly. Then reduce the heat to low and continue to cook, stirring constantly, until the glaze thickens and turns from opaque and cloudy to translucent, about 2 minutes. Remove the pan from the heat. Pour the glaze into a small bowl, cover, and chill it in the refrigerator for at least 4 hours or up to a day in advance.

Make the filling: In a medium-size bowl, mix the quartered strawberries with the chilled glaze. (The chilled glaze will have solidified to a Jell-O-like consistency, but stirring will loosen it substantially.) Set aside.

In a large bowl, combine the heavy cream and the confectioners' sugar. Whip the cream until it forms soft peaks. Fold in the vanilla extract.

Spread approximately ⅔ cup of whipped cream over the bottom of the graham cracker crust. (Reserve the rest of the whipped cream for topping the pie.) Gently pile the glazed strawberries on top, and chill the pie in the refrigerator.

Half an hour before you plan to serve it, remove the pie from the refrigerator so it can come to room temperature. Either mound the reserved whipped cream on the center of the pie or place a dollop on each of the individual slices.

Chocolate Raisin Pie

I love the combination of chocolate and raisins. From Raisinets to a divine raisin-studded chocolate coffee cake that my parents used to buy me as a treat, chocolates and raisins are a match made in heaven. So when I saw this recipe in Jean Hewitt's New York Times Heritage Cookbook, *I was more than a little excited.*

Jean Hewitt got started at the Times *in 1961 as an assistant to the venerable Craig Claiborne, head food critic for the paper. She went on to run the* Times's *test kitchen and to become a successful food writer in her own right, penning a number of cookbooks, four of which went on to win James Beard Awards.* Heritage *is a tome of a cookbook that explores the regional cuisines of the United States; it contains recipes for everything from soups, to casseroles, to the odd game dish, to breads, and, of course, to pies. First published in 1972, the cookbook is now out of print. If you ever spot a copy, I encourage you to buy it. The recipes recall dishes from another time—when food was not so processed and "fat" was not a bad word.*

The original recipe for this pie, as featured in Heritage, *came from Southern California, and I've stayed fairly true to it. I've altered only the amount of sugar (a little less) and the sort of chocolate used (semisweet). The pie is rich and sweet and, unlike most pies, actually gets better from sitting for a day.*

½ recipe Standard Pie Dough (page 28)

1¼ cups raisins
1 tablespoon all-purpose flour
1 cup heavy cream
2 ounces semisweet chocolate
4 tablespoons (½ stick) unsalted butter
2 large eggs
1 teaspoon vanilla extract
⅛ teaspoon ground cinnamon
½ teaspoon instant coffee granules
½ cup sugar
3 tablespoons cornstarch
Pinch of kosher salt

Place the raisins in the freezer and chill them for about 30 minutes (this will make them easier to chop).

Preheat the oven to 375°F.

On a well-floured surface, roll out the dough until it is about ⅛-inch thick and will fit a 9-inch pie plate. Gently pick up the dough, center it over the pie plate, and ease it into the plate. Trim the edges of the dough, leaving a 1-inch overhang. Fold the edges under, and then decoratively crimp the perimeter. Return the pie shell to the refrigerator to chill until the filling is ready.

Remove the raisins from the freezer and combine them with the flour in a small bowl. Toss well to coat. (The addition of the flour dries the raisins out a bit and makes them easier to chop.) Roughly chop the raisins either by pulsing them in a food processor or a blender, or by chopping them by hand with a very sharp knife.

Combine the chopped raisins, heavy cream, chocolate, and butter in the top of a double boiler. Place the pan over simmering water, and stir until the chocolate has melted. Remove the pan from the heat.

In a medium-size bowl, mix together the eggs, vanilla, cinnamon, instant coffee granules, sugar, cornstarch, and salt. Add this to the chocolate mixture, stirring to mix well.

Remove the pie shell from the refrigerator, and pour the filling into the shell. Bake for 35 to 40 minutes, until the filling is set. Shake the pie plate lightly to test this; the filling should jiggle only slightly. If the filling is not set yet, return the pie to the oven and continue to bake it for 5 to 10 minutes, checking it at 5 minutes. Remove the pie from the oven, and let it cool to room temperature before enjoying.

Pear Crumble Pie

The Northwest is pear country. Oregon and Washington grow nearly 80 percent of all the pears produced in the United States. They are one of the few fruits that don't need to tree-ripen to be delicious—you can bring home a rock-hard grocery store pear, set it on the kitchen counter, and have a succulent snack just a few days later. Given that, and the wonderful variety of pears available, it surprises me that they're so rarely used for pies. This single-crusted pie uses sweet, aromatic Anjou or Bartlett pears. Topped with a crumbly, buttery streusel, lightly spiced with a bit of cinnamon and ground ginger, it is a warm and homey pie—perfect for fall.

½ recipe Whole Wheat Pie Dough (page 40)

For the filling
2 pounds (about 4) pears, peeled, cored,
    and cut into ¼-inch-thick slices
Grated zest and juice of 1 medium lemon
¼ cup sugar
2 tablespoons all-purpose flour
Pinch of kosher salt

For the streusel topping
½ cup all-purpose flour
½ cup brown sugar
½ teaspoon ground cinnamon
½ teaspoon ground ginger

¼ teaspoon kosher salt
5 tablespoons unsalted butter, chilled,
cut into ½-inch cubes

Preheat the oven to 375°F.

On a well-floured surface, roll out the dough until it is about ⅛-inch thick and will fit a 9-inch pie plate. Gently pick up the dough, center it over the pie plate, and ease it into the plate. Trim the edges of the dough to leave a 1-inch overhang. Fold the edges under, and then decoratively crimp the perimeter. Return the pie shell to the refrigerator to chill until the filling is ready.

Make the filling: In a medium-size bowl, combine the pears, lemon zest and juice, sugar, flour, and salt. Toss gently until well combined. Set aside.

Make the streusel: In another medium-size bowl, combine the flour, brown sugar, cinnamon, ginger, and salt, and mix well. Add the butter and work the mixture with your hands, creating a rough, crumbly topping. Continue working and tossing the mixture, breaking down the butter into pea-size bits, until the topping resembles large, coarse crumbs.

Remove the pie shell from the refrigerator, and pour the filling into it, shaking the pie plate gently to distribute the fruit evenly. Pat the streusel evenly over the surface of the pear filling. The streusel should cover the filling.

Bake the pie for 40 to 45 minutes, until the streusel is golden brown and the juices are bubbling up through the surface. Remove the pie from the oven, and let it cool to room temperature before enjoying.

Meyer Lemon Cream Pie

I'm a native Californian, now residing in the Northeast. People out here seem to have some funny ideas about Californians. I will be the first to tell you, I'm not a surfer babe; in fact, the ocean rather scares me. Though I was always happy to be just a stone's throw from the redwoods, I never was much of a hiker. I never had any aspirations for the silver screen; I don't even go to the movies much. But there is one thing that's true about all Californians: we do come from a paradise where bountiful fruit trees grow right in our own backyards. One of my favorites is the fragrant Meyer lemon, a hybrid of a standard lemon and a mandarin orange, native to China, which was first introduced to the United States by Frank Meyer in 1908. Meyers are plump, thin-skinned, deep yellow in color, and much sweeter than standard lemons. The Meyer lemon has all the perfume of a lemon but almost none of the bite. Californians have been known to gobble them up thinly sliced, peel and all. Come winter, I enjoy them squeezed over fish, sliced and placed under the skin of a roasted chicken, juiced in a cocktail, and, of course, as the centerpiece of a delicious homemade pie.

This is an icebox pie, meant to be served straight from the refrigerator. A spicy gingersnap crust is the perfect complement to the bright, cooling cream filling. If Meyer lemons aren't readily available where you live, this pie is also wonderful made with good old standard lemons. Just increase the heavy cream to 1 cup in order to hit the right balance between tart and sweet.

1 Gingersnap Crust (page 44)

3 large eggs

¾ cup sugar

½ cup Meyer lemon juice (from approximately 5
lemons)

1 tablespoon cornstarch

Pinch of kosher salt

1 tablespoon grated Meyer lemon zest (from
approximately 3 lemons)

¾ cup heavy cream

In the top of a double boiler, combine the eggs, sugar, lemon juice, cornstarch, and salt. Beat lightly until blended. Place the pan over simmering water, and cook, whisking constantly, until the mixture has thickened and coats the back of a spoon, 5 to 7 minutes. (The curd will turn glossy and opaque when it's ready.) As soon as the curd is ready, fold in the lemon zest and remove the pan from the heat. Lay a sheet of plastic wrap directly over the surface of the curd to prevent a skin from forming, and allow it to cool to room temperature. When the curd reaches room temperature, place it in the fridge and chill it for at least 4 hours or up to a day in advance.

In a large bowl, whip the cream until it forms stiff peaks. Remove the chilled lemon curd from the refrigerator, and fold it into the whipped cream until the two are thoroughly mixed.

Pour the lemon cream into the prepared crust, shaking the pie plate gently to distribute the filling evenly. Return the pie to the refrigerator to chill for at least 1 hour before serving. If desired, allow it to sit for just 15 minutes at room temperature before serving.

BIBLIOGRAPHY

Beard, James. *James Beard's American Cookery.* Boston: Little, Brown, 1972.

Carey, Frank, and Jayni Naas. *The Kansas Cookbook.* Lawerence: University Press of Kansas, 1989.

Dague, Mary E., "Black Bottom Dinner Dance in Delight," *Wisconsin Rapids Daily Tribune,* 20 August 1936.

De Gouy, Louis Pullig. *The Pie Book.* New York: Dover Publications, 1974.

Edge, John T. *Apple Pie: An American Story.* New York: Putnam, 2004.

Egerton, John. *Southern Food: At Home, on the Road, in History.* New York: Knopf, 1987.

Farm Journal Food Staff and Nell B. Nichols, eds. *Farm Journal's Complete Pie Cookbook.* Garden City, N.Y.: Doubleday, 1965.

"Four Hundred at Cooking School Friday," *Van Nuys [Calif.] News,* 17 August 1933.

Green, Dymple. *Persimmon Recipes.* Mitchell, Ind.: Dymple's Delights, 1982.

Hatz, Aloah E., ed. *The Delaware Heritage Cookbook.* New Castle: Delaware Heritage Commission, 1987.

Hewitt, Jean. *The New York Times Heritage Cookbook.* New York: Putnam, 1972.

Hines, Duncan. *Adventures in Good Eating.* Bowling Green, Ky.: Adventures in Good Eating, Inc., 1937.

"Housewives of Valley End Course," *Brownsville [Tex.] Herald,* 22 November 1931.

La Ganke, Florence, "Nancy Page," *Laredo Times,* 6 December 1935.

Lewis, Edna, and Scott Peacock. *The Gift of Southern Cooking.* New York: Alfred A. Knopf, 2003.

Maddox, Mrs. Gaynor, "Hollywood Salad Recipe Is Culinary Scenario," *Ada Evening News,* 18 May 1937.

Malgieri, Nick. *How to Bake.* New York: HarperCollins Publishers, 1995.

McDermott, Nancie. *Southern Pies.* San Francisco: Chronicle Books, 2010.

McLagan, Jennifer. *Fat: An Appreciation of a Misunderstood Ingredient, with Recipes.* Berkeley, Calif.: Ten Speed Press, 2008.

Porter, M. E. *Mrs. Porter's New Southern Cookery Book, and Companion for Frugal and Economical Housekeepers.* Philadelphia: John E. Potter and Company, 1871.

Purdy, Susan Gold. *As Easy as Pie.* New York: Ballantine, 1985.

Robbins, Maria Polushkin. *Blue-Ribbon Pies.* New York: St. Martin's Press, 1987.

Seranne, Ann, ed. *America Cooks.* New York: Putnam, 1967.

Strause, Monroe Boston. *Pie Marches On.* New York: Ahrens Publishing Co., 1958.

Stuttgen, Joanne Raetz, and Terese Allen. *Cafe Wisconsin Cookbook.* Madison: University of Wisconsin Press, 2007.

Washington, Mrs. *The Unrivalled Cook-book and Housekeeper's Guide.* New York: Harper & Brothers, 1886.

INDEX